Town and Country Planning

The Report of a Committee of Inquiry appointed by the Nuffield Foundation

First published in 1986 by The Nuffield Foundation, Nuffield Lodge, Regent's Park, London NW1 4RS

ISBN 0 904956 25 3

Typeset by Exe Valley Dataset Ltd, Exeter, Devon
Printed by Henry Ling Ltd, The Dorset Press, Dorchester

"It would be inhuman pedantry to exclude
from the control of our development the
human factor. The human factor is always
present, of course, indirectly as the
background to the consideration of the
character of land use."

Lord Scarman in
Great Portland Estates plc v. Westminster LBC

Preface

The Nuffield Foundation has had a long standing interest in agricultural research and policy and hence in problems of land use. The present Inquiry arose from discussions with the Foundation's advisory committee on agricultural research and other experts about the possible long term conflicts over the use of land in the United Kingdom, which threw up questions about the principal means of making and implementing land use policy, that is the town and country planning system. Doubts were expressed about the system and touched not only on its mechanics but on the underlying political and economic assumptions on which it is based. Discussion revealed marked differences of view about the future of planning within government at all levels and within the planning profession. The aim of the Inquiry has been therefore not so much to gather facts as to elicit and articulate the different assumptions and values that inform the various views of planning and its future.

We began by canvassing the views of a dozen or so old planning hands about their experience of the planning system and from there branched out to consult informally with the major professional bodies, local government associations, developers and campaigning organisations. Some we commissioned to write for us, others volunteered both comments directed at our original brief (see Appendix I below) and other papers and reports germane to our concerns but written for other occasions. Some of these submissions concentrated on relatively short term problems and improvements to the system, but most attempted to grapple with the larger questions. What emerged clearly was a common view that the system has lost its bearings, but a reluctance to acknowledge that there is no consensus as to why this is so or what should be done about it. This impression was reinforced by the informal discussions which we subsequently held with planners, central and local government officials, developers and others. To that extent we were reassured that the Inquiry was well directed, though the way might be steep and the prospect daunting.

The Committee, which had met informally on several occasions, began its official existence in January 1983, with the following terms of reference:

> 'To inquire into the assumptions and purposes of the Town and Country Planning system, its past and present performance and its proper role in the future; and to report.'

By planning we mean the arrangements for plan making and

v

development control established by the Town and Country Planning Act 1947 and the modifications to those arrangements in subsequent legislation. To avoid the repeated use of the cumbersome term 'town and country planning' we refer simply to 'planning' throughout the report and where we discuss the wider notion of planning we refer to 'planning in general' or to 'economic and social planning'. We are of course aware that there is much other legislation whose purposes are closely allied to those of planning legislation proper, and we are indeed concerned about the nature of the relationship between them. When we refer to 'the planning system' we have in mind not only the arrangements for town and country planning, but the institutional structure in which they are embedded and the related arrangements for the management of the environment and of natural and other resources. We hope that this usage will make sense to our readers and that we have been tolerably consistent in employing it.

We have held 24 meetings and on 7 of those occasions invited others to join us in discussion of different aspects of the Inquiry. It has not proved possible to follow up all of the ambitious brief which we originally set ourselves. We were not able to pursue in any detail the question of the European context of planning and relied for international comparisons largely on the considerable experience of the Committee itself. While we do not make many explicit references to such comparisons, we have had them in mind. We have found, however, that we need look no further than Scotland for some of the practices which we think could most usefully be adopted throughout the United Kingdom.

There are a number of important questions on which we comment briefly but which we have not pursued. Our recommendations clearly have implications for the education and training of planners, but it will be for others to explore them. We decided at an early stage to resist the temptation to redesign the structure of local government, to leave aside the vexed questions of compensation and betterment, and not to get involved in detail with the Big Public Inquiry. Nor have we followed up the significant European developments on environmental impact assessments or on pollution control.

In our attempt to form some judgement on the performance of the planning system we have been struck by how little of the great body . of writing about it is based on quantitative research. It is not possible to say with any confidence, for instance, what have been the effects of planning policies on land prices. In the absence of a firm quantitative base, we are necessarily dealing in this Report with the analysis of informed opinion and drawing our own conclusions from it.

We gratefully acknowledge the help of all those individuals and bodies whose names are listed in Appendix II to this Report and would particularly like to thank four who wrote at our behest extended essays on particular subjects: Mr Anthony Barker on planning inquiries, Dr J K Friend on strategic planning, Mr Malcolm Grant on betterment and compensation, and Professor Nathaniel Lichfield on development control. We are grateful also to Professor Gerald Dix and his colleagues at the University of Liverpool for generously keeping us supplied during the course of the Inquiry with issues of the *Town Planning Review*. A number of practical difficulties have prevented us from following up all the offers of help which we received. For that we can only apologise and hope that somewhere in our evidence are reflected the views of those we were unable to consult directly.

In the early stages of the Inquiry we relied much on the guidance of Sir Wilfred Burns, whose death robbed us of a wise and congenial counsellor and the only professional planner on the Committee. We were fortunate that Mr F J C Amos agreed to serve in his place and to bring to our deliberations his wide experience of planning and local government.

Finally we are glad to pay tribute to those whose help has made this Report possible: to Dr Barry Pearce who undertook the formidable labour of analysing the evidence and produced the bulk of the initial draft on which the Report is based; to Mr John Ardill who at a late stage in the Inquiry helped most ably to fill in the background; to Miss Lesley King, Miss Elizabeth Sellé and Mrs Julia Hum, who acted successively as secretaries to the Committee and organised its meetings with patience and good humour; and especially to Mr James Cornford, Director of the Foundation, who strove against all odds to keep the Inquiry on an orderly course and quite beyond the normal call of duty wrote the final draft of this Report.

Flowers

Membership of the Committee of Inquiry

Chairman

Rt Hon the Lord Flowers FRS
  Vice Chancellor of the University of London;
  Trustee of the Nuffield Foundation

Members of the Committee

F J C Amos CBE
  Formerly Chief Executive, Birmingham City Council;
  Past President Royal Town Planning Institute
  (member of the Committee from March 1984)

Sir Wilfred Burns CBE
  Formerly Chief Planner, Department of the Environment
  (died January 1984)

Rt Hon the Lord Butterworth CBE
  Formerly Vice Chancellor of the University of Warwick;
  Trustee of the Nuffield Foundation

Professor Gordon Cameron
  Professor of Land Economy, University of Cambridge

Glyn England F Eng JP
  Chairman Council for Environmental Conservation;
  Dartington Institute;
  Formerly Chairman Central Electricity Generating Board

Professor Jeffrey Jowell
  Professor of Public Law, University College, London

Professor Sir Hans Kornberg FRS
  Professor of Biochemistry, University of Cambridge;
  Master of Christ's College, Cambridge
  Trustee of the Nuffield Foundation

Sir Frank Layfield QC

Professor J P W B McAuslan
  Professor of Law, University of Warwick

Professor R C O Matthews CBE FBA
  Professor of Political Economy, University of Cambridge
  Master of Clare College, Cambridge
  Trustee of the Nuffield Foundation

Roger Warren Evans FCIOB
   Managing Director, Demos Group;
   Formerly Director, Swansea Centre for Trade and Industry
Sir Ralph Verney Bt KBE
   Formerly Chairman, Nature Conservancy Council

Secretariat:

Mr J P Cornford
Dr B J Pearce
Mrs J Hum

Contents

PART III   ANALYSIS

PART IV   CONCLUSIONS

Introduction

Since 1979 the government has taken or proposed a number of steps which have been widely interpreted as a concerted attack upon town and country planning. These include the introduction of enterprise zones, simplified planning zones and urban development corporations, the restriction of the scope of development plans, an increase in the extent of permitted development under the General Development Order, further proposals to change the General Development Order and the Use Classes Order, the abolition of the metropolitan counties, modifications to the green belt, individual decisions to permit development against the wishes and the approved plans of local authorities, and commitment to major projects—the Channel Tunnel and Canary Wharf—without prior consultation with planning authorities or subsequent public inquiry into their implications for land use. Whether or not these measures have been concerted, they have certainly not been the subject of considered public investigation and deliberation. They reflect a strong belief that the planning system has become too slow and too rigid, that it is a major obstacle to economic regeneration, and that its scope and the degree of discretion it affords to local planning authorities should be curtailed.

There are contrary views and it is one main purpose of this Report to examine and distinguish them. For it is not simply a case of less planning or more, but of what kind of planning and for what purposes. If we look back to the proximate origins of the present system, we can see that four cardinal assumptions embodied in the 1947 Town and Country Planning Act have been called into question or indeed abandoned in the intervening years. The first of these was that the task of planning is to control and direct in the public interest spontaneous private development. In many parts of the country there is no such development to direct and the task of planning has been redefined to assist in creating development. Secondly it was assumed that planning control was necessary to protect the countryside from the encroachment of the town, but not from the impact of its own major industry, agriculture, as many now think necessary. Thirdly, while in the era of post war reconstruction local authorities were expected to combine land use planning with their own ambitious investment plans, it was assumed that other public agencies would pursue their programmes in the public interest without the discipline of development control. Lastly the system was also designed to ensure that decisions on

1

planning permission would have no effect on the value of land: this assumption or principle was the first to be abandoned and the problem of how to apportion between community and developer the gain from planning permission has remained a political football since 1953. We can no longer take for granted that there will be a demand for development, that the agricultural industry is an adequate guardian for the countryside, that the intentions of public sector developers will mesh harmoniously with the plans of local authorities, or that gain will accrue to the community.

Uncertainty about basic assumptions and criticism of the practical effects of the system have led us to start at the beginning and to sketch out in some detail in Part I of this Report the changing context and content of planning since 1947 and its reflection in legislation. In Part II we examine rapidly the arguments for and against planning as such, a variety of views on the faults of the system as it now is and an equal variety of views on how to change it for the better. Despite searching criticism of the costs and effectiveness of planning, there remains a conviction that land is a unique resource and that the control of development is both justified and necessary to protect amenity, to ensure the provision of public facilities, and to conserve natural resources, the landscape and our cultural heritage. Intervention in the market is also advocated to reduce uncertainty and temper rapid changes, and to eliminate on ethical grounds intolerable material conditions, discrimination and antisocial activities.

All these are seen as matters on which planning may rightly touch and which ought to influence decisions about land use. The system is widely seen to fall short of these requirements, because it has been too much concerned with the physical environment at the expense of wider social and economic considerations. It is said not to provide the coordination necessary between land use and other kinds of planning; between local planning authorities, statutory undertakers and central government; and between the various functions of local government. It has failed to improve environmental quality and to engage with major issues such as industrial decline, the management of the countryside, and the conservation of natural resources.

Critics find the planning system unsatisfactory because of the persistent failure of successive governments to make clear statements of national policy as a framework for local plan making. Nor is there an adequate means to deal with regional problems. The structure is inappropriate because of the division of functions between counties and districts, the location of boundaries and the proliferation of special agencies. Present regulations and procedures are an obstacle to good planning: too much detail is

2

prescribed by central government, the preparation of development plans take too long, likewise their approval, plans are more like blueprints than guidelines and there are too many regulations. Public participation is ineffective and the public inquiry favours the strong at the expense of the weak. The planning profession finds itself in a position of increasing political exposure for which it is ill-prepared.

In Part III we analyse these views at greater length in order to isolate what we see as the major dimensions of disagreement: from the possibility of a politically neutral system and the role of the market to the scope for public participation and the proper role of the planning profession. From these disagreements we see emerging not two opposed views of planning, but seven which reflect differences of priority, development against conservation, different experiences, growth against decline, different aspirations, consumption against participation, different interests, accumulation against redistribution, and so forth.

Finally we come to our own prescriptions which do not quite coincide with any of the seven views we have attributed to others. In our view planning should be both more and less ambitious. More ambitious by bringing within its scope all those in the private and public sectors whose activities have implications for land use. Less ambitious in that however far ahead planners are obliged to look, they must acknowledge the uncertainties in which they have to work and regard all plans as tentative, requiring continual revision. The primary purpose of the institutional arrangements for planning should be to increase both the obligations and the incentives for all the actors, central and local, public and private, to share information about their future intentions, and in this way to increase the chances that damage to the environment can be prevented, waste and confusion minimised, conflicting demands for land reduced, and development assisted. We are not convinced that this will best be achieved by dismantling the present system, by reducing local discretion and by a reliance on a combination of the market and occasional intervention by central government. On the contrary we believe that given the great differences in conditions across the country, what is required is an extension and strengthening of the discretion of local planning authorities within a framework of consistent and clearly articulated national policy. If there is an urgent reform required in the planning system it is for central government to put its own house in order.

There are national policies which must take precedence over local choice and we believe that the onus is on central government to make these policies explicit. At present it does not do so and the policy vacuum at the centre leads to national waste where

3

departmental policies conflict and to local waste where the plans of local authorities fall foul of unspecified national policy. This policy vacuum is most readily apparent and damaging in such fields as energy, agricultural land, transport and the inner city. We believe that statements on the lines of the Scottish national planning guidelines would go some way to fill the void.

Some other mechanism is also needed to bring together central and local decisions at the regional level, to improve communication and to help to resolve conflicts. We do not believe that this requires the creation of a further tier of government and instead suggest a possible scheme for handling regional problems within the existing government structure.

Though we advocate a wider role for planning it is certainly not our intention to suggest that planning should become synonymous with government. The point is that planning should take into account the gamut of government activity insofar as it affects the environment. At national level this ought to produce a greater degree of coherence between departmental policies. At local level it would allow individual authorities to make their own decisions about priorities between the environment, the economy and social welfare. Wider scope for planning would give local authorities the opportunity for intervention beyond their existing powers. We think that any such power carries an obligation to exercise greater restraint and to improve the effectiveness of local accountability in practice, by providing greater public access to plan making, decisions and inquiries.

As we say at the beginning of Part IV what we want of a planning system is that it should include all bodies, public and private, whose activities have significant implications for land use; that it should encourage the exchange of information among such bodies; that it should use this information to identify and if possible resolve potential conflicts of land use; that it should provide local diversity within a national framework; that it should be accessible to those affected by its decisions; and that it should recognise the inevitable limitations on planning far ahead and be flexible, adaptable and modest in the face of uncertainty. As is usual different members of the Committee place different weight on its various recommendations, but we hope that all of them suggest direct and practical ways in which these characteristics may be encouraged.

PART I BACKGROUND

Chapter 1 The Context and Content of Post War Planning

1.1   The British land use planning system is founded on a block of wartime and post war legislation centred in the 1947 Town and Country Planning Act. Its origins can be traced through a number of intertwining strands of circumstance, theory, practice and law.

1.2   The legislative background was provided by a series of public health and housing acts which began in the middle of the last century in response to public concern about the insanitary and congested conditions in the burgeoning towns and cities of the industrial revolution, the associated poverty, and the moral consequences of these factors. The first to incorporate the term 'planning' came in 1909, the Housing, Town Planning, etc Act, which encouraged the building of working class housing in urban and rural areas and empowered local authorities to make 'town planning schemes' to regulate the layout of new developments in the interest of sanitary conditions, amenity and convenience. The 1909 Act and subsequent amendments were repealed by the Conservative government's 1932 Town and Country Planning Act which extended the making of schemes to all land, developed or undeveloped, but in a less thoroughgoing way than was envisaged in a Labour administration bill the previous year.

1.3   The establishment of this rudimentary legislative framework was accompanied, and outstripped, by the evolution of planning theory and a growing voluntary planning movement, marked by 19th century model industrial settlements like New Lanark, Saltaire and Bourneville, and culminating, in this period, in the garden cities of Letchworth and Welwyn. The garden city concept, which gained wide currency, was reflected also in Hampstead Garden Suburb and, in the public sector, by schemes like Manchester's Whythenshawe development. In spite of the provision for schemes, however, most development—characteristically sub-urban accretions, ribbon development along major roads, and industrial estates—escaped the influence of planning.

1.4   The interwar years of depression, mass unemployment and migration to the South East brought official measures to promote industrial development in the depressed areas which represent the beginnings of a regional element in the planning system. They also brought a growing concern about the economic, social and environmental consequences of industrial and urban concentration, heightened at that time by fears of vulnerability to air attack, which prompted demands for a more comprehensive planning system.

1.5   These strands were drawn together by the Barlow Commission on the Distribution of the Industrial Population, which was appointed in 1937 and reported in 1940. The report recommended the redevelopment of congested urban areas, the decentralisation or dispersal of industries and industrial population, and the encouragement of a reasonable balance and diversification of industry throughout the regions. It commended as the means of achieving these aims the development of garden cities, satellite towns and trading estates and the further development of small towns and regional centres. Subsequent reports dealt with some of the key issues raised by Barlow: Scott on rural land; Uthwatt on compensation and betterment; Reith on new towns, Dower and Hobhouse on national parks and access to the countryside.

1.6   The 'foundation' acts derived from these reports include the Minister of Town and Country Planning Act 1943, the Town and Country Planning Acts of 1944 and 1947, the Distribution of Industry Act 1945, the New Towns Act 1946 and Town Developments Act 1952, and the National Parks and Access to the Countryside Act 1949.

1.7   The post war town and country planning system was born in hope and confidence. The reports of Barlow, Scott and Uthwatt had identified the problems and the remedies. There was general agreement, among politicians, planners and the public, on the need for action and the objectives to be attained. Industry and population were to be decanted from the congested conurbations to new and expanding towns in their rural hinterlands. The economic and social balance between the depressed industrial regions and the too rapidly growing South East and West Midlands was to be restored. Good agricultural land which had been swallowed up by the unplanned growth of London and other conurbations and which was now needed to feed the nation was to be protected. The wilder and more beautiful areas of countryside were to be protected too, along with the livelihood of their inhabitants, but also opened to the public for outdoor recreation. New homes were to be built in better, more spacious surroundings with new schools, hospitals, shops and playing fields.

1.8 The experience of war had created the right climate for this radical departure. Basic industry, weakened by the interwar depression, was back at work but had to be restored to a peacetime footing. Bomb damage made the redevelopment of inner city housing and industrial areas and city centres both more urgent and more feasible, presenting the nation with both the need to act and the opportunity to create a better environment. The war had brought planning and rationing, the efficient use and distribution of available resources, into every aspect of life; and it had been seen to work. The refurbishment of Britain's physical fabric and renewal of its infrastructure slotted in beside the refurbishment of its economic, social and intellectual fabric. The redistribution of economic activity among its regions sat comfortably beside the redistribution of wealth and opportunity among its people at large.

1.9 There were doubts about the adequacy to the task of the governmental machinery. The 1943 Act had created a new central government department, the Ministry of Town and Country Planning, to set up and oversee the system but at the local level the existing planning machinery was administered by 1,441 local authorities. Many local government functions—gas and electricity, health and social security—were transferred by the post war Labour government to new ad hoc agencies and it was suggested that the new planning system too should be placed with special agencies. In the event, local government retained responsibility but only at the level of the 146 county and county borough councils. Much of the responsibility for achieving national planning objectives was, however, placed with specialised agencies. Development corporations were established outside the framework of local government to plan, build and manage the new towns. Responsibility for redistributing and fostering industrial growth was placed with the Board of Trade and remained largely outside the formal land use planning machinery. Local authorities were given their part to play through their redevelopment of existing urban areas, slum clearance and housebuilding.

1.10 The role of the local planning authorities, the county and county borough councils, was to assist this public development, redevelopment and relocation of settlements by identifying and setting aside the necessary land and drawing up master plans for the physical layout and provision of infrastructure. The statutory tools were the development plan and powers to control all private development.

1.11 The plan, a series of documents and maps based on a survey of the area, set out how the authority proposed land should be used and the stages by which development should be carried out over a period of 20 years, subject to ministerial approval and a quinquennial review. Once approved, the plan was intended to provide the framework not only for positive development by the local and other public authorities but also for the control of private development in the interests of good neighbourliness and amenity and of meeting national and local objectives.

1.12 Much of the early optimism was misplaced, however, as the whole process found itself handicapped from the start by a variety of factors. In the early years there was a scarcity of resources: money, manpower and construction material. Both at the centre and in the local authorities the planners had to compete with more deeply entrenched professions, particularly the transport, architecture and housing establishments which resisted the claims of planning to interfere in their fields. Local authorities had to draw upon surveyors and engineers whose background and outlook tended to dominate the newly emerging planning departments. Moreover, the local planning authorities, the putative coordinating agencies, had little control over the land use activities of other public authorities. Development by the Crown, including government departments, health authorities and industrial estates corporations, did not need planning permission while developments by statutory undertakers and local authorities which required the authorisation of a government department—for loan sanction or grant aid, for example—were under the relevant legislation 'deemed' to have planning permission when such consent was given. Developments by local planning authorities which conformed with an approved development plan could also be deemed to have planning permission. These factors contributed to a serious lack of coordination both between and within the various levels and types of public agency which, to some extent, has continued to prevail.

1.13 The history of town and country planning over the last 40 years reflects the interplay of economic, social and demographic changes, the alternation of political control and philosophy at national and local level, and the evolution of planning theory and practice. Changes in policy, practice and legislation have tended to follow, and often lag behind, the events which gave rise to them. The operation of the system has moreover been regularly and strongly punctuated by ad hoc advisory plans and government initiatives conducted outside the system. Ad hoc regional studies and strategies have provided the main link between land use planning and regional economic planning which were brought closer together for a short period in the late 1960s and early 1970s but have generally remained distinct.

New towns

1.14 The principal source of planning policy and practice, following Barlow, was indeed a collection of non-statutory advisory plans for Greater London, the Clyde Valley, the North East and other areas drawn up during and after the war. The Greater London Plan (GLP) of 1944, prepared by Professor Patrick Abercrombie (who was an influential member of the Barlow Commission, and author of two dissenting reports) proposed a reduction of more than one million in the population of the area which stood at some 8.6 million in 1939, having grown by two million between the wars. Over 600,000 were to go from Inner London (covered then by the London County Council) which would be redeveloped at a lower density. Some 380,000 were to be decanted to eight new towns with populations between 30,000 and 50,000 while another 260,000 would be housed in urban expansion schemes. The plan foresaw some 250,000 people moving out of the conurbation on their own initiative.

1.15 Fourteen new towns were begun between 1946 and 1950. Not all were designed to accommodate overspill from parent cities. Peterlee in County Durham was for the resettlement of mining communities; Corby in Northamptonshire to service steel works built before the war to exploit local ore deposits. Nor were they all entirely new settlements. Some of the areas chosen for London overspill already had substantial populations.

1.16 The administrative arrangements and principal master plan parameters for the new towns were recommended by the Reith Committee and embodied in the 1946 Act. Established by statute, appointed by the government, funded by the Treasury, outside the planning control of local government, new town corporations were empowered to acquire, hold, manage and dispose of land, to provide services, carry out any business or undertaking and do anything else 'necessary or expedient' for the purposes of the new town. These arrangements, and the fairly constant support of central government, gave the new towns a coherence, consistency, continuity and single-mindedness lacking in local government sponsored development.

1.17 On principles derived from the garden city concept, the new towns were laid out as a cluster of residential neighbourhoods, each with a small local centre and basic amenities, separated from one another and arranged around a town centre, with separate areas zoned for industry and commerce, all the parts giving relatively easy access to each other. From the start, the allocation of houses was related to the provision of jobs. Initially these were mainly in manufacturing industry, creating an imbalance in the employment structure. There was also, in the early years, a dearth of social amenities. These factors, and particularly perhaps the strangeness of a new and deliberately planned settlement in the eyes of people coming from old established communities, contributed to a poor public image of the new towns, especially in the 1960s when planning in general was losing its appeal.

1.18   By the late 1960s the London new towns had virtually met Abercrombie's population targets, although they had not met his objective of stabilising London's population. By then a second wave of new town development was under way, attached mainly to middle-sized freestanding towns like Warrington, Peterborough and Northampton. The 28 new towns now in existence have added just over a million people to the original populations of the designated areas, and created within those areas nearly half a million extra jobs.

Regional policy

1.19   The war ended the mass unemployment which, in part, had prompted the establishment of the Barlow Commission and begun the process of relocating industry which Barlow recommended. The 1945 Distribution of Industry Act gave responsibility for continuing the task not as Barlow had suggested to a new national agency but to the Board of Trade (BoT). The Act also redefined the special areas designated before the war for government aid and renamed them development areas. Within these areas the BoT was empowered to build factories, make provision for public services and reclaim derelict land. Treasury grants and loans were made available for specific industrial undertakings. The inducements to industry to locate in the development areas were reinforced by restraints elsewhere. Factory building everywhere was controlled by a building licence system introduced during the war. The licencing system was supplemented and eventually replaced by the system of industrial development certificates (IDCs) introduced in the 1947 Town and Country Planning Act. IDCs had to be obtained, as a prerequisite of planning permission, for any factory development of more than 5000 sq ft.

1.20   The application of regional policy was slackened in the early 1950s but revived towards the end of the decade, only to break down again in the mid 1970s. Frequent changes in the focus and application of policy brought uncertainty both for industrial developers and the local planning authorities. In 1958 elements of regional aid were extended to additional, smaller areas defined by unemployment rates (Distribution of Industry (Industrial Finance)

Act, 1958). This new basis was taken for the redefinition of assisted areas as development districts in 1960 (Local Employment Act, 1960), giving a wider geographical coverage, including some rural areas, but bringing even greater uncertainty as changing unemployment rates moved areas in and out of the assisted category.

1.21 A new era began in 1963 with the publication of white papers on the two most economically depressed regions, Central Scotland (A Programme for Development and Growth. Cmnd No.2188. HMSO 1963), and North East England (A Programme for Development and Growth. Cmnd No.2206. HMSO 1963), designating eight growth areas in the former and a growth zone in the latter where economic development was to be fostered by public investment as well as regional aid, divorced once again from the unemployment criterion. The unemployment test was abandoned generally in 1966 when extended development areas, covering 40 per cent of the country, were created. The following year additional priority was given to a number of special development areas. The fiscal tools of regional policy were changed several times during this period and were supplemented by the introduction of a regional employment premium giving direct subsidy for the first time to labour costs. Over the same period policy was extended to the rapidly growing office sector, first by encouraging offices to relocate outside central London, then by the application of office development permits, initially in London, later throughout the South East, East Anglia and the Midlands.

1.22 Regional policy in the 1960s found a new rationale in the belief that development of the underused resources of the regions could contribute to national economic growth. It also came under the influence of new theories, adapted from French practice, of indicative planning and growth poles. With the emphasis on public investment and infrastructure provision, derelict land reclamation and other environmental improvement measures, economic and land use planning were drawn closer together at a time when land use planning itself was facing new stresses and undergoing reassessment.

1.23 Although it created some new jobs, and ameliorated the effects of economic change, in the assisted areas, and probably helped to stem population drift to the South East and Midlands, regional policy did not significantly correct economic imbalances. While assisted areas received more than their share of new factory building, particularly during periods when regional policy was rigidly applied, they did not enjoy a corresponding concentration of new jobs. Nationally the growth in employment, from the mid 1950s

11

onwards, took place in the service sector which was not initially subject to controls. Nor did regional policy tackle the more fundamental weaknesses in the organisation and structure of the primary and secondary industries, which were first disguised by the post war boom and then exacerbated by growing foreign competition, inflationary pressures and periodic recession. Regional policy may indeed have contributed, by restraining growth and innovation, to the decline of the manufacturing sector which, between 1966 and 1982, suffered a net loss of 2.75 million jobs (33 per cent).

1.24   In the recent years of economic depression, growing unemployment and accelerated changes in industrial structure, disparities between the depressed and prosperous regions have remained and have extended to previously successful regions like the Midlands. However the maldistribution of economic activity between regions has been supplanted as the focus of national policy by the growing problem of industrial decline, unemployment, and social deprivation in the inner cities, a problem affecting London and Birmingham as well as the northern conurbations, whose inner areas had benefited little from regional policy.

Local authority planning and development

1.25   The first thrust of post war public development came, as we have noted, from the new town development corporations which were set up rapidly, before the main framework of statutory planning was in place. The local authorities were slower to respond, in both positive development and statutory plan making, hindered by a range of factors including a collapse of the post war consensus, an unanticipated growth in population and prosperity, and a failure first to appreciate and then to grapple with the complexities of comprehensive planning.

1.26   Slow progress by the county and county borough authorities in preparing the 1947 Act development plans was matched by tardiness at the centre in approving them. It was 1961 before all the English and Welsh authorities had approved plans. Manchester's, approved that year, was by then in need of reappraisal. It had been submitted in 1951 on the basis of 1945 study. Coventry, in the forefront of planning authorities, fared little better: the plan submitted in 1951 was approved in 1957 and revised in 1962.

1.27   The development and redevelopment schemes of local authorities were also slow to bear fruit. Implementation was hindered by the lengthy and cumbersome process of land acquisition by compulsory purchase, a problem exacerbated as time passed by rising land prices, limited local authority resources, and changing circumstance. Councils gave too little attention to the resources needed to implement their proposals. There was also, in the early years in particular, too great an expectation of what planning could achieve; too little appreciation of the obstacles it was likely to encounter. The preparation, assessment and re-preparation of positive development plans for some places extended over a period of decades, while development proceeded piecemeal or not at all. Those plans which were completed too often solidified in concrete and brick a pattern of development which was already becoming outdated. Others fell victim to their inadequacy before they were put into effect. Private enterprise increasingly took over the lead, but only where development was profitable and where it could be accommodated by the planning authorities.

1.28   Once the first wave of new town development was fully launched, the emphasis on relocational housing was passed back, by the first post war Conservative government, to the local authorities. The 1952 Town Development Act provided for agreed schemes for the expansion of existing towns to house overspill population from the conurbations. The development could be carried out by either the exporting or the host authority.

1.29   In 1955 the government gave emphasis to the concept of green belts (Ministry of Housing and Local Government Circular 42/55), long current in planning theory, as an instrument of urban containment. Local planning authorities were asked to consider designating belts of land several miles wide to check the further growth of large urban areas, prevent neighbouring towns coales-cing, or preserve the special character of a town. Development, except for appropriate rural uses, was to be permitted only in very exceptional circumstances.

1.30   This initiative coincided with a new start on slum clearance, neglected since the start of the war, a continuing rise in the birth rate, and an increase in new household formation. Local authorities estimated that 850,000 unfit houses needed clearing and aimed to deal with 378,000 by 1960 (but achieved the clearance of only 260,000 by that date).

An era of change

1.31   In the early 1950s too there was a renewed emphasis on private sector development. In 1953 the Churchill government abolished the development charge (Town and Country Planning Act, 1953), which was introduced in the 1947 Act as part of the attempt to divorce planning decisions from land values. The restoration of value in planning permissions was a stimulus to the private sector, a hindrance to the public sector, and a temptation to corrupt practices. The growing private sector activity also shifted the focus of local planning authority activity away from plan making to development control, which became increasingly seen by the public as a bureaucratic and negative process. Moreover this shift took place more often than not in the absence of approved statutory plans, which were supposed to provide the framework for development control.

1.32   These events coincided with, and in part reflected, a period of rapid change in British society for which the planners were unprepared. Migrational movement occurred on a larger scale than anticipated. Conurbations continued to grow at the periphery even as overspill and redevelopment policies reduced the numbers in the inner cities. They then began to lose population to their surrounding areas beyond the green belts, more as the result of private sector suburban development than by planned overspill in new and expanding towns. The population of the home counties grew by 800,000 in the 1950s, a third of the net population growth in Britain as a whole.

1.33   Aided by the green belt policy, shire counties resisted the efforts of conurbation authorities to secure overspill sites, giving rise to some monumental battles fought out at public inquiries. The difficulty in securing sites, the adoption of more generous internal space standards and the provision of more public open space and communal facilities, the structure of public sector housing finance, and the introduction of new and largely untested building techniques combined with other factors to produce multistorey blocks as the predominant form of council house building in the inner cities.

1.34   As austerity gave way to increasing prosperity there was a strong and growing demand for housing—and more spacious housing—for consumer goods and cars. Throughout the 1940s and 1950s the growth of car ownership and traffic constantly exceeded official estimates. Residential areas, pre or post war, did not cater for car ownership on this scale. Few houses had garages and there was little parking space. Nor were existing main roads able to cope with the increased commuting, shopping and leisure motoring which was stimulated not only by greater car ownership but also by the lack of employment, retail and social facilities in many of the prewar suburbs and post war housing areas. Restrictions on capital expenditure ensured that few road improvements were put in hand and although a great deal of highway planning was carried out it was 1955 before a major construction programme was begun, including the motorways which had been advocated by county surveyors in 1938.

1.35   The 1960s brought a plethora of responses to these mounting problems. 1961 saw the publication of the Parker Morris Report (Ministry of Housing and Local Government Central Housing Advisory Committee: Homes for Today and Tomorrow. HMSO 1961) on housing standards, providing for more generous and more flexibly laid out internal space and better basic facilities. In the same year the government announced the designation of the first of a new wave of new towns at Skelmersdale to relieve the housing pressure on Merseyside, and began a series of regional planning studies. The South East Study (South East Study 1961-81. HMSO 1964), published in 1964, forecast a need to house a further 3.5 million people in the region between 1961 and 1981, arising largely from natural growth, immigration from abroad, and an influx of retired people to the south coast. Its proposals for further new towns, at Milton Keynes and attached to the existing towns of Northampton, Peterborough and Southampton, were largely adopted. Similar findings and solutions emerged from the West Midlands and North West Studies.

1.36   These exercises coalesced with the economic plans for Central Scotland and the North East, referred to above, to give birth to further regional studies and strategies produced after 1965 by the newly appointed economic planning boards and councils, either by themselves or in conjunction with local authorities. The Strategy for the South East (HMSO 1967) was reworked by the planning council in 1967 and by another ad hoc team jointly commissioned by the council and the standing conference of local planning authorities in 1968. Ad hoc teams were appointed also for the North West (Strategy Plan for the North West. HMSO 1974) and North East (Strategy Plan for the Northern Region. HMSO 1977) strategies which progressively advanced the analysis of land use and economic needs of the regions in terms of the available and necessary resources. Rather more limited strategies were produced in the other regions. The focus of the strategies varied between economic and physical planning issues from region to region. That for East Anglia (Strategic Choice for East Anglia. HMSO 1974), had a strong rural orientation.

1.37   In 1963 the Buchanan Report (Ministry of Transport: Traffic in Towns. HMSO 1963) was published, establishing the vital link between land use and transport planning. In the 1950s the number of vehicles had doubled to more than nine million. Buchanan

15

forecast that the number would increase to 27 million by 1980. (In the event the 1980 figure was 18.6 million.) The Report made clear the massive scale of road building, and consequent urban re- structuring, that would be needed if society were to give free reign to traffic but argued that provision could be made on a lesser scale if traffic was curtailed to a corresponding extent. The central concept of Buchanan's solution was a system of primary road networks to cater for the free flow of through traffic and 'environmental areas' where inessential traffic would be discouraged or prohibited. The Report also advocated the incorporation of transportation plans into the statutory town and country planning system. Many of the Report's ideas passed quickly into general currency. Trans- portation studies were commissioned for several of the major conurbations. Transportation planning, coordination of public transport, and traffic management measures were incorporated in subsequent legislation.

Structure planning

1.38   In 1964 the shortcomings of the 1947 development plan system were subjected to the scrutiny of an official Planning Advisory Group (PAG) (The Future of Development Plans: A Report by the Planning Advisory Group. HMSO 1965). The Group found that it had become increasingly difficult to keep statutory plans up to date and responsive to the demands of change. Its report the following year recommended a two part system, intended to speed up the plan making process, increase its flexibility, and broaden its scope. The system, incorporated in the 1968 Town and Country Planning Act, comprised a structure plan which as before required ministerial approval and a series of local plans which needed only to be adopted by the planning authority. The structure plan was intended to be a broad brush exercise, describing the authority's strategic policies not only for land use and associated transportation systems but also for achieving its wider social and economic objectives. It was to be a written document whose proposals could be illustrated dia- gramatically but not delineated precisely on a map. Map-based local plans were to elaborate the general proposals and set out development control policies for either a limited area of compre- hensive change (action areas) or for larger localities (district plans). A third class, subject plans, was to deal with specific policy issues such as housing, mineral workings or conservation.

1.39   The adoption of structure planning coincided with the general acceptance of new planning theories. Hitherto the accepted method of plan making was to survey the area, analyse its known or foreseeable problems, pressures and demands, and produce a plan which described a state of affairs expected or desired at some future date. The new theories adopted a continuous, cyclical, systems approach based on the identification of needs, formulation of goals, the identification and evaluation of alternative courses of action and the monitoring and readjustment of adopted programmes. Such theories, variously expressed, were applied by the joint teams and consultants who carried out the many sub-regional planning and transportation studies which preceeded the formal introduction of structure planning (just as the 1947 Act had been preceeded by Abercrombie's GLP and other regional advisory plans).

Local government reorganisation

1.40   It was envisaged that structure plans should express the policies of the local planning authority within the context of national and regional policies and objectives. The system was designed ideally for a structure of all purpose local authorities each covering a cohesive rural or urban area whose land use and transport systems could be planned as a whole. It did not therefore fit well into the current hybrid structure of all purpose county boroughs, upper tier counties and lower tier county districts, the latter in turn enjoying a variety of powers, including some delegated planning functions, according to whether they were non-county boroughs, urban districts or rural districts. Most of their boundaries had long ceased to reflect the pattern of urban growth. The conurbations, in particular, were mosaics of differing sizes and types of local authority. But London local government had already been reorganised in 1963 (London Government Act, 1963) on the metropolitan pattern, with a strategic authority covering, more or less, the whole of the built up area, and large boroughs to provide the personal services. It was generally expected, when Royal Commissions were appointed in 1966 to deal with the rest of the country, that they would produce a system suited to structure planning.

1.41   The Royal Commission on Local Government in England, chaired by Lord Redcliffe-Maud (Cmnd No.4040. HMSO 1969), indeed recommended a system of 58 unitary authorities for most of the country with metropolitan structures for the Merseyside, Greater Manchester and West Midlands conurbations. All, including Greater London, were to be grouped under eight provincial councils whose main responsibility would be for strategic plans setting the framework and order of priorities within which the local authorities would work out their planning policies and major investment programmes. The Wheatley Commission (Royal Com-

17

mission on Local Government in Scotland. Cmnd No.4150. HMSO 1969), recommended a two tier system of regions and districts.

1.42   The reports were accepted by the Wilson government in 1970 but the Redcliffe-Maud proposals were replaced by the Heath government in 1971 with a less radical alternative. The metropolitan solution was adopted for six conurbation areas. Elsewhere many of the existing counties were retained almost intact, although smaller ones were merged and new counties were created on the Tees and Humber estuaries and the English side of the Severn estuary. District authorities were reorganised into larger units with common status. Metropolitan districts differed from the less populous shire districts in having a larger range of functions, with a corresponding loss of functions at the upper tier. But in both the metropolitan and shire systems planning was divided. Structure planning was given to the upper tier, local planning and development control mainly to the lower level. This system was brought into effect in England and Wales by the 1972 Local Government Act. The Wheatley proposals were enacted for Scotland the following year. The question of provinces in England was left to the Kilbrandon Commission (Royal Commission on the Constitution. Cmnd 5460. HMSO 1973), but its recommendations for regional coordinating and advisory councils were not acted upon.

1.43   The reformed planning system devised by the PAG was thus brought within a reformed system of local government with which it was fundamentally incompatible. The new local government boundaries in England and Wales were not drawn primarily to encompass cohesive areas for land use and transport planning. The retention of a two tier structure divided not only the town and country planning function but also the service functions of local government which the PAG had intended should be embodied within structure plans. The best fit, from the structure planning viewpoint, was achieved in the shire counties which are responsible for education, social services, highways, refuse disposal, and libraries. In the metropolitan areas, however, education, social services and libraries are with the district councils, and everywhere housing is a district function. In this fragmentation lay the seeds of continued dispute between county and district levels, and of the eventual abolition of the metropolitan counties.

1.44   Attempts were made nevertheless to integrate planning with other functions within each authority. The new councils were recommended to set up corporate management and planning systems and were required to prepare formal plans and investment programmes for transport and housing. The adoption of a corporate approach, in policy-making and management, did much to bring land use planning into a central, and pivotal, role in local administration.

An era of uncertainty

1.45 Local government reorganisation had been preceded by a reorganisation of central government departments which created in 1970 the Department of the Environment (DOE), bringing together planning, housing, transport and other areas of environmental control and management. As in the immediate post war years, problems had been identified and a new start made, and there was a certain amount of, and again in the event misplaced, optimism. The first Environment Secretary, Peter Walker, gave improvement of the environment as his top priority and talked of creating 'a new age of elegance', and the Minister for Local Government and Development, Graham Page, said that structure plans were being pushed forward so vigorously that the logjam would disappear in a matter of months.

1.46 The name of the new department reflected the growing public consciousness of and concern about the environment in its every aspect: the conservation of buildings, townscapes, landscapes and wildlife; the damage caused to the ecosphere and human health by pollution; the deterioration in the quality of life resulting from traffic congestion and from noise on the roads and at airports; and the new perception that finite natural resources imposed limits to population and economic growth. But public satisfaction with the results of positive planning and confidence in the capacity of the planning system to solve problems were now sinking. Pressure groups were growing, in number and energy. The public was beginning to challenge planning policies and decisions with more vigour, not so much through the new statutory machinery for participation in plan making introduced by the 1972 Act as at public inquiries, particularly those into major schemes like roads and reservoirs and, notably, into the site for a third London airport. Increasingly the public inquiry, which was designed to let those directly affected by development proposals voice their objections, was seized upon as an opportunity to question or denounce national policies.

1.47 There was also at this time a growing concern among planners, social scientists and politicians, about the social and economic consequences and redistributive effects of planning. It focussed in particular on the inner city areas where housing redevelopment was sweeping away the corner shops and small businesses which provided employment, local services, social cohesion, and a local authority tax base. Housing redevelopment at lower densities was also contributing to rather than solving a growing housing shortage. Urban planning strategies, which had been aimed from the time of Abercrombie onwards at creating a better quality of life in the inner cities, appeared instead to be creating pockets of multiple deprivation.

1.48 These changes in the framework of development plans, in planning methods, in planning authorities, and in the perceptions of what planning was doing and failing to do coincided with changes in demographic and economic trends. A central objective of planning since 1947 had been to reduce the populations of the major conurbations, but on an assumption that without planning policies they would continue to grow. By 1961, however, most of the conurbations were experiencing severe population decline and, although it only later became evident, an even more severe decline in employment. Growth was shifting for a variety of reasons to smaller towns and rural areas. In Greater London, whose population fell by over 500,000 between 1961 and 1971 to 5.45 million, the decline in manufacturing industry was above average and although this was partially offset for some time by the growth of service industries, that sector also saw an absolute decline between 1974 and 1981. The fall in population and employment was accompanied by changes in the age structure and the structure of the work force in inner city areas, which exacerbated the problems.

1.49 Between 1964 and 1974 the national birthrate fell dramatically. Taken with other demographic factors, including a reduction in Commonwealth immigration which had hitherto tended to hide the underlying trends in some of the conurbations, this led to a virtually stable population. In the early 1960s all regions had a growing population. In the following decade a number of shifts became apparent. Between 1971 and 1981 the population of the Northern and North West regions and Scotland fell and that of the South East was virtually static. The biggest changes were all on the growth side: the population of the East Midlands grew by 5.64 per cent, that of the South West by 6.7 per cent, and East Anglia's by 12.6 per cent.

1.50 The coincidences of change are encapsulated in the history of the Great London Development Plan (GLDP) which the Greater London Council (GLC), created in 1963, was required to prepare as a planning strategy for the area. (It was later redesignated a structure plan, in line with the 1968 Act.) The plan, best known for its three concentric motorway boxes (which attracted 90 per cent of the objections at public inquiry), was completed in 1969. By then council officials already recognised that its provisions were no longer appropriate to the changing circumstances. While it proposed a planned reduction in the metropolitan population, that population was already falling at a faster rate than envisaged, and in ways which seemed likely to distort the social fabric and fiscal base. Its policies did not fully address the economic and social problems of the area. They were also at odds with those proposed in the South East Strategic Plan (SESP): the GLDP aimed to retain employment in the metropolitan area; the SESP to disperse it around the region. The plan was rewritten by the GLC in terms of broader social and economic objectives while the public inquiry into its original provisions, which lasted from 1970 to 1972, was taking place. A third version was produced by the Inquiry Panel. A further version was produced, and approved, by the DOE in 1976 (Greater London Development Plan: Statement and Report of Studies; GLC 1969. Statement Revisions; GLC 1972. GDLP Report of the Panel of Inquiry (Layfield Report) 1973).

Economic decline and urban decay

1.51   The creation of the new local authorities coincided also with the end of the period of economic expansion. Early in their existence the new authorities were warned by the Wilson government that they must begin to curb their expenditure. Subsequently the Thatcher government reinforced exhortation with general reductions in the level of rate support grant, expenditure ceilings and penal withdrawals of grant aid. With end-of-the-century population forecasts reduced from over 70 million to 58 million, the Wilson government also announced that the new town programme would be wound up and resources redirected to the inner cities. As the manufacturing base and the pool of potential new industry shrank, regional policy went into decline. In 1977 the regional employment premium was abolished. In 1979 the incoming Thatcher administration cut both the amount of regional aid and the size of the assisted areas, and abolished the economic planning councils and the Location of Offices Bureau. It also announced that it would make no response to the North East Regional Strategy, the last and most sophisticated of the regional studies, which was based on a thorough analysis of the region's economy, including the incidence of public expenditure. Other regional strategies were equally ignored. A certain amount of regional coordination has continued by the voluntary collaboration of local planning authorities, notably the Standing Conference of London and South East Planning Authorities (SERPLAN).

1.52   In the mid and late 1960s inner city policies were directed towards improvements in housing, education and the social services. The urban programme, as it was then known, was progressively widened, with an increasing emphasis on participation by the voluntary sector. In 1977, with the publication of a white paper (Policy for the Inner Cities. Cmnd No.6849. HMSO 1977), the scope was further enlarged to embrace industrial, environmental and recreational provision. At the same time the role of overall coordination of a wide variety of inner city related programmes was transferred from the Home Office to the DOE. Selected local authorities were given powers to declare improvement areas and to stimulate economic activity by loans and grants for industrial buildings. The present administration has heightened the emphasis on private sector initiatives, and has sought to encourage this by a relaxation of planning controls. Under the 1980 Local Government, Planning and Land Act it has established enterprise zones where development which falls within predetermined limits does not require specific planning consent, and established urban development corporations with similar powers to new town development corporations.

1.53   Inner city policy has effectively replaced regional policy as the governmental response to economic and social disparities. The inner city problem however has not so much replaced as overlain the regional problem. Scotland, Wales and Northern England continue to suffer higher unemployment, a poorer industrial structure, a less skilled workforce, and fewer locational advantages than the South. The South East, apart from Inner London and a few isolated pockets, continues to have a preponderance of service and high technology industries and research establishments and the locational advantages which will be enhanced by the completion of the M25 ring around London, the development of Stansted airport, and the Channel Tunnel.

Urban conservation

1.54   Both in the inner cities and in the country at large the emphasis has changed over the past 20 years from new development to the preservation and renovation of existing buildings and built up areas. Like the new town and garden suburb concept, the preservation movement is voluntary in origin and predates statutory planning. The Society for the Preservation of Ancient Buildings was founded in 1877, the National Trust in 1895. The Ancient Monuments Act was passed in 1882, and has been amended on several occasions. Under current legislation any work on monuments scheduled by central government requires consent.

Under planning legislation the government also maintains lists of buildings of special architectural or historic interest which may be demolished or materially altered only with the consent of the local planning authority. Local planning authorities may also compulsorily purchase listed buildings which are deliberately neglected. Preservation was extended from individual buildings to entire districts under the 1967 Civil Amenities Act, a private member's measure sponsored by the Civic Trust. It gives local planning authorities the duty to designate conservation areas within which they must pay special attention in all planning decisions to the preservation or enhancement of the special historic or architectural character and appearance. The measures have been widely applied to residential districts, villages, town centres and the shopping and business areas of cities.

1.55 Economic and social considerations have promoted the preservation of ordinary houses and buildings without special historic or architectural merit. Grants for housing improvement have been available since 1949 but were not taken up in any number until the mid 1950s. By the late 1950s improvements were running just behind demolitions. The availability of grants encouraged the middle class 'gentrification' of many inner city districts of Georgian and Victorian housing, with a consequent loss of accommodation in these areas for working class families. In the mid 1970s government policy moved on from the improvement of individual houses to an area-based strategy of comprehensive gradual renewal in which stress was placed on economic and social factors as well as the physical fabric of buildings. Provision was also made for individuals and community groups to become involved in the process. In both housing improvement and conservation areas there has been widespread adoption of the 'environmental area' traffic management concepts introduced by the Buchanan Report.

1.56 Grants and improvement policies have not prevented a deterioration in the national housing stock now reaching crisis proportions, and extending to many post war council housing estates. The government, having applied a brake to public expenditure on housing improvement by the 1980 Housing Act which channelled resources to properties and owners most in need, is currently encouraging private sector involvement in the refurbishment of such estates.

Agriculture and the countryside

1.57 The principal land use in Britain, agriculture and forestry, has a special relationship with the planning system. The loss of agricultural land to uncontrolled urban development, and the consequent loss of capacity to meet the nation's food needs, was a major consideration in the setting up of the post war planning system. The Scott Report on Land Utilization in Rural Areas suggested that prospective developers should make out a clear case of national advantage before planning permission was given. Thus while agriculture and forestry have been left free from development control, the protection of agricultural land from non agricultural uses has been one of the primary objectives of the planning system since the foundation acts. Restated in DOE Circular 75/76, which reflected concern at the amount of farm land then being taken for housing, industrial and recreational use, government policy is 'to ensure that, as far as possible, land of a higher agricultural quality is not taken for development where land of a lower quality is available and that the amount taken is no greater than is reasonably required for carrying out development in accordance with proper standards'.

1.58   The Ministry of Agriculture, Fisheries and Food (MAFF) grades land according to the degree to which its physical characteristics limit its agricultural use. On the best land in grades 1 and 2 which make up 17 per cent of the agricultural land in England and Wales, there is a strong presumption against other uses. Grade 3 land, comprising 50 per cent of the total, is subdivided into categories 3a, 3b and 3c, with fairly strong presumptions against development on 3a and 3b. Land graded 4 and 5 is of severely limited agricultural use.

1.59   Open countryside has however represented the main land resource for urban and economic growth: for new and expanding towns, for major industrial plans, for roads, airports and reservoirs, and for minerals. As the 1976 circular admitted 'development and agriculture are competitors for land and it is often the better quality land which is the most suitable for building'. Planning authorities, with the backing of agricultural interests and country-side conservationists, have been largely faithful to the presumption against development, and many of the principal development bids have been decided on appeal. The annual loss of agricultural land, estimated at around 40,600 acres at the time of the 1976 circular, has now fallen to less than half that figure. Since 1979 the Thatcher government has increasingly encouraged the use of derelict and underused urban sites as an alternative to the development of rural 'greenfield' sites.

1.60   The foundation acts and subsequent legislation also put strong emphasis on protecting the beauty, character and public

24

amenity of rural landscapes. Today more than 15 per cent of the total land area of England and Wales is covered by ten national parks and 36 areas of outstanding natural beauty, within which there are stronger policies against development. Protection is also extended to some 200 national nature reserves and over 4,000 sites of special scientific interest covering about 3.5 million acres. Other locally adopted protection policies greatly extend the areas subject to restraint on development, although the degree of protection afforded and the rigour with which controls are applied varies. It is estimated that in the South East region more than 80 per cent of undeveloped land is covered by policies which carry a strong presumption against development. Proposals for development within protected areas, whether by the private sector or public agencies, invariably meet with fierce resistance from conservation and environmental pressure groups. Protection is not absolute and development does take place where local or national needs are held to be of overriding importance.

1.61   In the absence of planning controls over agricultural and forestry operations, however, many old-established landscape features and natural or semi-natural habitats have disappeared. In 1984 the Nature Conservancy Council reported in 'Nature Conservation in Great Britain' (NCC 1984), that 95 per cent of lowland neutral grasslands lacked significant wildlife features, 80 per cent of chalk and limestone grassland was lost or significantly damaged, 40 per cent of lowland heath on acidic soils was lost, 30 to 50 per cent of ancient lowland woodland was lost, 50 per cent of low lying wetlands and 30 per cent of upland heaths and bogs were lost or significantly damaged, and 120,000 miles of hedges had been removed. There is now strong pressure for the imposition of development control.

Green belts—constraint and conflict

1.62   The presumption against development conveyed by green belt policies is not intended primarily to protect agricultural land but to stop urban sprawl. The concept of a buffer zone around settlements to prevent their endless expansion and convergence derives from the garden city movement and was taken up in the foundation reports. It was introduced in law by the 1938 Green Belt (London and Home Counties) Act which empowered the relevant local authorities to acquire land for green belt purposes and to add to it private land whose owners were willing to forego development. The main impetus came in 1955 however from Ministry of Housing and Local Government Circular 42/55 which asked local planning authorities to consider submitting sketch plans for green belts

25

several miles wide to check the further growth of a large built up area, prevent neighbouring towns from merging into one another or preserve the special character of a town. Inside a green belt, the circular said, approval should not be given except in very special circumstances for the construction of a new building or change of use of an existing building for purposes other than agriculture, sport, cemeteries, institutions standing in extensive grounds or other uses appropriate to a rural area. Existing towns and villages within the green belt should not be allowed to expand except by strictly limited infilling or rounding off. Further advice on drawing boundaries was given in another circular in 1957 (Ministry of Housing and Local Government Circular 50/57). It recommended the use of suitable landscape features—roads, streams etc—for outer boundaries and said the inner edge would mark a long term boundary for development. It also recommended that pockets of land between the built up area and green belt which might be developed later should be marked as 'white' land, and added that strict control in green belts should not result in permission being given elsewhere for development inappropriate or detrimental to the countryside.

1.63   A number of the subsequent submissions were rejected by government and all those approved were amended to allow some peripheral development. Partial approvals resulted in a two tier system of formal and interim green belt areas, the latter including most of the innermost sections. Development has continued within the designated and interim areas, particularly in the London green belt where growth has been only marginally less than in designated growth areas. Development pressures have been exacerbated in recent years by the relatively greater economic success of smaller towns. The M25 motorway ring around London, nearing completion, is an additional growth magnet.

1.64   The future of the green belts is now one of the most vigorously debated issues in planning. A 1983 draft circular by the then Environment Secretary, Mr Patrick Jenkin, positing some relaxation of restraint, met with fierce opposition from pressure groups and Conservative MPs and councillors in the Home Counties. The House of Commons Environment Select Committee declared that green belts should be sacrosanct. The circular finally published in July 1984 (DOE Circular 14/84) reaffirmed the objectives of the 1955 circular but added to the checking of urban sprawl the role of 'safeguarding the surrounding countryside from further encroachment and assisting in urban regeneration'. Giving additional guidance on the drawing of boundaries in local plans, it added that the essential characteristic of green belts 'is their permanence' and 'their protection must be maintained for as far as can be seen ahead'.

1.65 Intense pressure for sites for modern high technology industry, out-of-town shopping centres and housing is in conflict with this policy. House builders who maintain that structure planning authorities and the government are not allowing enough land to meet market demand are challenging the 'sanctity' of the green belt, notably by proposals for complete new townships within or close to the London green belt. There is equally intense resistance by shire counties to additional housebuilding either in the green belt or in areas previously subject to growth policies. They are supported in this not only by conservationists but also by London local planning authorities which want to see development concentrated in their areas. The government, in a housing land circular (DOE Circular 15/84), issued simultaneously with that on green belts, asked local planning authorities to take account of the market demand and bring forward an adequate supply of land. It also urged them to make use of neglected, unused or derelict urban land. Under powers in the 1980 Local Government, Planning and Land Act it maintains a register of such sites in public ownership and can enforce their disposal. Urban Development and Derelict Land Grants are available to help make such land suitable for development.

The challenge of rural change

1.66 The countryside at large has had to bear the burden of many planning and economic initiatives basically related to urban and industrial problems and needs—new and expanding towns, motorways, airports, reservoirs, energy supplies, mineral workings, and recreational space. It has been subjected to the opposing forces of conservation policies and of rapid change in agricultural methods. It has not however been favoured to anything like the same extent by positive planning measures. There was an unspoken assumption at the time of the foundation acts that areas of countryside untouched by planning policies could look after themselves.

1.67 It is now becoming evident that policies aimed at protecting rural land against urban incursions and at concentrating public and private investment in urban areas into designated key settlements have worked against industrial development and other employment opportunities elsewhere in the countryside, leading to low wages, population drift, and a consequent loss of services and amenities. The shift of economic growth from the conurbations and large cities to smaller towns and rural areas is a comparatively recent phenomenon and many rural communities, particularly those in the uplands and more remote areas, continue to suffer economic decline and social deprivation. Green belt, national park and other restraint policies have put a premium on housing values, attracted those who can afford the prices, and acted to the detriment of poorer indigenous populations. There is no satisfactory mechanism in the planning system to ensure that private sector housing is reserved for locally generated needs. Recent attempts by the Lake District Planning Board to impose such restrictions on builders have been overturned on appeal. Restraints on industry and mineral extraction in such areas similarly reduce employment opportunities.

1.68 Increased mechanisation, and now automation, of farming has meanwhile reduced employment in agriculture. Farming, moreover, is now falling victim to its own success and the success of national and EEC policies of increasing output and protecting markets. Mounting food surpluses are forcing a reassessment of policies which could lead to between 15 and 30 per cent of British agricultural land becoming redundant. No agreed strategy for reducing surpluses has yet emerged from the EEC and the extent to which it will act, the way in which it will act, and the consequences of such action remain a matter of speculation. The threat of drastic change has however forged a new alliance between farming and landowning interests, conservationists and rural community organisations. A consensus has emerged in favour of a package of measures to diversify farming activity by public support for landscape and habitat conservation, public access and recreation, and new economic activities. A marked increase in afforestation is among the other prospects being canvassed, along with the adoption of new non-food crops such as chemical and pharmaceutical feedstocks and biomass for energy, for which as yet no clear market has been identified.

1.69 The British government is beginning to respond to such pressures. The Ministry of Agriculture is currently promoting in an Agriculture Bill powers to designate environmentally sensitive areas where grants will be payable to farmers maintaining traditional agricultural practices or conserving landscapes and habitats. In January 1986 the Minister for the Environment, Countryside and Local Government, Mr William Waldegrave, in a speech to farmers, indicated a new involvement by his Department in agricultural affairs. It had responsibility, he said, for some of the policies which were bound to be needed to supplement agricultural policy. It 'must look to the needs of the rural community as a whole as well as to planning and conservation issues'. At the same time he restated the traditional approach to countryside planning, declaring that the 'real war' for environmentalists was to 'limit the permanent loss of countryside to urban and industrial development' since land going to waste would quickly be taken up by 'cheap housing, the aggregate industry, waste dumping, and all the other alternative uses of large tracts of land'.

1.70   Within days the Ministry of Agriculture announced that it would seek, in the Agriculture Bill, new statutory responsibilities to strike a 'reasonable balance' between a stable and efficient agriculture, the economic and social interests of rural areas, conservation of the natural beauty, amenity and flora and fauna of the countryside and the promotion of public enjoyment of the countryside. A year earlier the government had resisted an almost identical clause, drafted by pressure groups, in a private member's measure, the Wildlife and Countryside (Amendment) Act. The Ministry subsequently reorganised its Land Division to take account of these wider responsibilities and set up a new policy unit to deal with alternative uses for land.

The current scene

1.71   The immediate post war consensus on planning objectives — the consensus on which the planning system was founded—has largely disappeared. National objectives have swung to and fro with changes in government, giving varied emphasis to the part to be played in development by the public and private sectors, but with perhaps only one major shift, the return to a free market in land. Policies have changed also in response to changing circumstances and new perceptions. The pace of development, of housing, roads and public infrastructure generally, has also been varied from time to time as a means of regulating the economy. The planning system itself, however, although it has been overhauled and extended, although it has been criticised as cumbersome and unwieldy and blamed for many failures, although it has been at the centre of many battles, has remained for most of its existence largely outside national political controversy.

1.72   At the local level, land use planning has been drawn more into the centre of policy making and administration through the introduction of structure planning which was specifically designed to incorporate broader social and economic objectives in the planning process, and the adoption of the corporate planning and management approach. It has also become more deeply embroiled in the increasing politicisation and polarisation of local government. Since local government reorganisation the proportion of councillors sitting as representatives of national political parties, rather than as independents or ratepayers associations, has increased, particularly in the shire areas, and local party organisations have come to play a stronger role in council affairs. Many more councillors have become full time professional local politicians. The political spectrum has widened and there have been more frequent changes of political control, both between parties and between factions within parties. More recently the advance of the Liberal/SDP Alliance has resulted in a number of councils without any overall political majority. At the same time many pressure groups involved in planning, environmental and social issues have also become politicised. Some local government officers, too, have become more overtly and actively political. Pressure groups and the professions have interacted, and both have provided councillors. These trends have resulted in the planning system being harnessed to ideological ends, and have brought uncertainty and instability to its operations. This is not to suggest that planning is always and everywhere the object of political conflict. In many places councils are by consensus and in collaboration with the local community using development control powers to enhance the appearance of their areas as a matter of civic pride.

1.73 The planning system as an element of local administration is essentially a tool for managing growth by the coordination in space and time of various programmes and activities. Over the past decade, against a background of reduced financial resources, including lower levels of central government grant aid, falling local tax bases and central controls on spending, the decline of regional policy, and a shortage of potential developers, particularly in the industrial field, local authorities have increasingly been using planning as a tool to promote growth. Building on experience gained in the 1960s and 1970s in town centre redevelopment, they have been forming partnerships with the private sector and bargaining with developers for planning gains in the form of job creation, environmental improvement and payment for infrastructure in return for grants of planning permission.

1.74 The Thatcher government has encouraged partnership arrangements, particularly in inner city areas where it has promoted collaborative efforts between the local authorities, the private sector and voluntary agencies by grants and specific programme initiatives. More generally however, it has acted to reduce the scope and lessen the controls of planning as part of its drive to draw back the frontiers of state intervention by deregulation and privatisation.

1.75 Declaring a 'fierce determination to halt and reverse the decline in the economy', which he attributed in part to the planning system, the new Conservative Environment Secretary, Mr Michael Heseltine, told planners in 1979 that the system was trying to do too much. He had no intention of wrecking the system. It was required for conservation, for protecting land with a special purpose, such as agriculture and minerals, and as a basis for development control. But it must be streamlined. Structure plans should not contain every conceivable matter of interest to a county council, and their revision should not be preceded by vast surveys. Local plans where needed should be prepared quickly and approved in advance of the relevant structure plan. Development control should be speedier and more responsive. In the 1980 Local Government, Planning and Land Act which his speech foreshadowed, this streamlining process was begun. Most development control responsibilities allocated to county councils under previous legislation were reallocated to district councils and an 'expedited procedure' for local plan adoption was introduced. The Act also gave powers to set up urban development corporations with local planning authority functions to regenerate inner city areas, and enterprise zones where development conforming to a predetermined scheme does not need individual permission and is exempted from rates and certain taxes. It established registers of unused or underused land owned by public bodies, the sale of which can be enforced by ministerial direction. Fees for planning applications were introduced for the first time.

1.76 A 1980 circular (DOE Circular 22/80) asked local planning authorities to use the development control system to facilitate development, and always to grant permission 'unless there are sound and clear cut reasons for refusal'. Small businesses, particularly in rural areas and in redundant buildings, should not be refused planning permission simply because the area was zoned for other uses. Enforcement action should be taken against breaches of planning control only where planning reasons clearly warranted it. Amendments in 1981 (SI 1981 No.245) and 1986 to the General Development Order widened the limits within which minor extensions may be made to houses and factories without planning consent. New regulations for structure and local plans were introduced in 1982 and elaborated in a 1984 circular. The abolition in 1986 of the GLC and the six English metropolitan county councils removed the strategic planning tier in the major conurbations.

31

1.77 The government's intentions to continue the process of simplifying and improving the efficiency of the planning process were reaffirmed in a 1985 white paper 'Lifting the Burden' (Cmnd No. 9571. HMSO 1985). The Housing and Planning Bill now before Parliament contains powers for local planning authorities to set up Simplified Planning Zones, similar in scope to Enterprise Zones but without the fiscal inducements, and for the government to give urban regeneration grants to private sector bodies for improvements and developments in inner city areas. It also contains further measures for speeding up the planning process.

1.78 The government is also proposing amendments to the Use Classes Order which governs the extent to which the use of property can be changed without planning permission. After strong representations from local planning authorities, amenity bodies and others, the government has however abandoned a more radical liberalisation of the Order recommended by the DOE's Property Advisory Group.

1.79 There are certain elements of internal conflict in the land use and economic policies being pursued by the present government, and of conflict between those policies and emerging socio-economic trends. This is most evident in relation to housing where the government wants the private sector to take the lead and market forces to be accommodated, yet is constrained by existing policies and commitments from giving the market free play. Its policy of maintaining the green belts and other countryside protection measures, backed by considerable electoral pressures, runs counter to the clear indications of demand for new housing in rural settings outside the conurbations. There are similar demands from modern high technology industry which makes up one of the most buoyant sectors of the economy. Government sponsored infrastructural investments like the Channel Tunnel, the M25 and the expansion of Stansted as London's third airport will add to these pressures and conflicts and may exacerbate regional disparities in the current absence of a positive regional policy. The considerable effort to stimulate inner city redevelopment as a means of tackling deep seated economic problems and defusing growing social unrest is a further, related intervention in the market. These has been no attempt to study, let alone tackle, inner city problems in the wider context of conurbation, regional and national economic, demographic and land use issues.

1.80 Over all this hang two unresolved questions: what will happen in the countryside if vigorous measures are adopted by the

European Community to curb farm surpluses? And what changes will be brought about in patterns of employment and its locational needs by the information technology revolution? While it may not yet be possible to answer these questions it is increasingly evident to some observers that the issues are interrelated and that they form the essential context for an eventual reassessment of the national distribution of population and economic activity as fundamental as that carried out by the Barlow Commission.

Chapter 2   The Legislative Framework

2.1   The British town and country planning system as established by the foundation acts and subsequent legislation comprises in essence three elements:

(a)   A system of statutory plans indicating what development is intended to meet the needs of the planning area over a given time, and where development is to be permitted, refused or otherwise subject to special conditions;

(b)   A system of controls to ensure that development is carried out in accordance with plans, policies and statutes;

(c)   A system of governmental and quasi-governmental agencies to administer the planning and development control functions and to secure development.

2.2   The 1947 Town and Country Planning Act which brought into being the system of statutory plans and controls was amended in 1951, 1953, 1954 and 1959, and the ensuing body of law was consolidated in the Town and Country Planning Act 1962. A new style of plan making was introduced in the 1968 Town and Country Planning Act and there was a further consolidating measure in 1971. Although there has been a good deal of subsequent amendment, including the 1981 Local Government, Planning and Land Act, which simplified the plan-making procedure and reallocated development control functions, the 1971 Act remains the principal act relating to town and country planning in England and Wales. The Scottish system has some differences which are described at the end of this chapter.

Development plans

2.3   The 1947 Act required each local planning authority to survey its area and to prepare on that basis a development plan indicating how it proposed land should be used, by development or otherwise, and the stages by which development should be carried out. The plan was intended to show which towns and villages were suitable for development and which could best be kept at their present size, the direction in which a city would expand, areas to be kept as agricultural land, areas for housing and industrial development, the sites of proposed roads, public and other buildings and works, airfields, parks, pleasure grounds and other public open spaces, and nature reserves. The plan, which could be for all or part of the authority's area, was to be submitted to the responsible minister within three years for approval, with or without his amendment, and was to cover a period of 20 years, subject to quinquennial review.

2.4   The plan consisted of a series of documents and maps: a report of the survey; a written statement with accompanying basic map; other maps and descriptive material elaborating and illustrating the plan. The additional maps might show the proposals for a specific town or development area. Before approving the plan the minister was required to assess its general provisions, to hold a public inquiry at which objectors could be heard, and to consider the inquiry inspector's report. Once approved, the plan provided the basis not only for positive development by the local authority but also for the control of private development. It did not however guarantee the right to carry out any development indicated in the plan, nor did it provide the only yardstick by which such decisions are taken.

2.5   Local planning authorities were empowered to propose amendments at any time and required to review the plan, on the basis of a fresh survey and analysis, after five years. In practice no more than half the initial plans had been approved by 1955 and the last was not approved until the early 1960s. The delays and other difficulties encountered in the operation of the system led to the appointment in 1964 of the Planning Advisory Group (PAG) whose report the following year recommended a new system incorporated in the 1968 Town and Country Planning Act and consolidated in the 1971 Act. This system, which remains in force, consists of two parts: a structure plan which as before requires ministerial approval and local plans which require only to be adopted by the local planning authority.

Structure plans

2.6   Once again, the local planning authority was required to carry out a survey of the area. The Act specifices that the survey should examine the area's principal physical and economic characteristics; the size, composition and distribution of the population; the communications, transport system and traffic; other considerations bearing on these issues; other matters the minister may prescribe or direct; and any changes already projected in the above matters and the effect they are likely to have on the development or planning of the area. All these matters are to be kept under review.

2.7 Unlike the earlier development plan, the structure plan prepared on the basis of this survey is not intended to be a precise, mapped indication of development intentions. It must be a written statement:

(a) Formulating the local planning authority's policy and general proposals in respect of the development and other use of land in that area (including measures for the improvement of the physical environment and the management of traffic);
(b) Stating the relationship of those proposals to general proposals for the development and other use of land in neighbouring areas which may be expected to affect that area; and
(c) Containing such other matters as may be prescribed or as the minister may in any particular case direct.

2.8 The authority is required to ensure that the policy and proposals are justified by the result of the survey. It must also have regard to current policies for the economic planning and development of the region as a whole, and to the resources likely to be available for carrying out the proposals. Although no map is required the plan is to be accompanied by 'appropriate diagrams, illustrations and descriptive matter'.

2.9 With ministerial consent, separate plans may be prepared for different parts of the structure planning authority's area. The authority must when preparing the plan give adequate publicity to the report of survey and the matters to be included in the plan and opportunity for objections. The draft plan must be made available for public inspection when it is submitted for approval.

2.10 The minister can return the plan for further action if he is not satisfied that the authority has adequately publicised and consulted on its proposals. If he is satisfied he can either approve it, in whole or in part, with or without modifications or reservations, or reject it. In doing so he must take account of any matters he thinks relevant, whether or not they were taken into account in the submitted draft. If he does not intend to reject it he must consider any objections and hold an examination in public of those matters he considers affect his consideration of the plan.

Local plans

2.11 The 1968 Act assumed planning would be carried out by unitary authorities which would elaborate the broad strategy of their structure plans in a series of local plans. The 1972 Local Government Act, however, allocated structure planning to county authorities and local planning primarily to the district authorities, while requiring the county to prepare a development plan scheme describing the local plans to be made and which authorities should be responsible for them.

2.12 Local plans comprise an ordnance survey based map, a written statement and illustrative material. They are meant to develop the policy and general proposals of the structure plan and relate them to a precise area of land, to provide a detailed basis for development control and for coordinating the development and other uses of land, and to bring local and detailed planning issues before the public. The 1971 Act prescribed two kinds of local plan: action area plans dealing with areas designated in the structure plan for comprehensive development, redevelopment or improvement; and district plans covering the whole of a substantial area. Planning authorities may also prepare subject plans dealing with specific policy issues such as housing, mineral workings or conservation, which need not be precisely mapped. The device has been adopted mainly by shire county planning authorities which were responsible for 41 of the 54 subject plans deposited by the end of 1984.

2.13 The local planning authority must ensure that the plan proposals conform generally to the structure plan as it stands, whether or not it has been approved, and must have regard to any information or other considerations it considers relevant or the minister specifies or directs. The authority must give adequate publicity to its proposals, consider representations during preparation of the plan, and allow objections to the completed plan, which may be considered at a public inquiry. The authority, in adopting the plan, does not have to take account of objections. Nor does the plan need ministerial approval. The authority must however send the draft plan to the minister who may direct that it should not take effect unless approved by him. Just once, in 1986, has a planning minister rejected a local plan (Southwark London Borough Council's North Southwark Plan) having first directed that it should not be adopted. The authority can alter, repeal or replace the plan, subject to the minister's approval if he has decided the original plan.

The present position
2.14 It was envisaged that structure plans, setting out strategic policies which did not need to be precisely located on a map, would be prepared and approved more quickly than the old style development plans. In the event they too have proved to be a lengthy and elaborate process. By 1979 only 57 of the 72 required structure plans had been submitted, and only 27 approved. It was 1985 before every area had an approved structure plan.

38

2.15 In an attempt to speed up the process, the Thatcher government altered the procedure for preparing and adopting structure and local plans by the Local Government, Planning and Land Act 1980.

2.16 A ministerial memorandum of 1984 (DOE Circular 22/84), explaining the Act, said that structure and local plans should 'provide the necessary framework for development control and direction of development'. It continued: 'structure plans give a general indication of where development should be located and its scale; local plans provide detailed locations for the future supply of land for housing and industry, define the boundaries of areas of restraint, and coordinate development programmes. The end product of the plan making process should be a clear and concise statement of policies and proposals for development which strike a satisfactory balance in land use between immediate availability, for various kinds of development, and safeguarding for future contingencies and conservation. To be useful, structure and local plans should be monitored and kept up to date and easy to grasp and to interpret. They should avoid undue rigidity and policies should be sufficiently flexible to cope with minor variations. The plan making process itself provides authorities with positive opportunities to reassess the needs of their areas, resolve conflicting demands, consider new ideas and bring forward appropriate solutions'.

2.17 Structure plans, the memorandum added, should be limited to policies and general proposals of structural importance which control particular types of development in the whole or a substantial part of the area, indicate the scale of provision to be made in the area and the major locations for development, and indicate the general location of individual developments likely to have a significant effect on the area. They should take account of national and regional policies as they affect the physical and environmental planning of the area and should provide the framework for local plans.

2.18 The Act provided that a structure plan's written statement should no longer include a reasoned justification for its policies and proposals, this being relegated to an explanatory memorandum which does not form part of the plan. The examination in public, required before approval of initial structure plans, became discretionary for proposals to alter, repeal or replace them. While the Act allows authorities to prepare action area plans, structure plans revised under the Act are no longer permitted to define such areas. The Act introduced an 'expedited procedure' by which the local planning authority may seek a ministerial 'direction' to adopt or alter a local plan in advance of the adoption or alteration of the structure plan. The circular described the circumstances in which alterations to an approved structure plan were appropriate. It asked planning authorities to keep their development plan schemes up to date, providing a programme of plan preparation for the next two to three years. It stressed that plans are not necessary in all areas.

2.19   By December 1984, 323 local plans had been adopted and a further 245 were awaiting adoption. The majority were district plans. Some 30 per cent of local planning authorities, mainly shire districts, had not yet deposited any plans. Many local planning authorities rely on, or supplement formal plans by, informal plans and policy documents.

Development control

2.20   Development control is the means by which local planning authorities seek to put their development plans and policies into effect. It constitutes the principal day to day occupation of planning departments and committees, and is the point at which individuals and organisations most frequently come into contact with the planning system.

2.21   In the prewar system of planning schemes, development was permitted or prohibited by the zoning of land for particular uses. The post war legislation not only introduced a more flexible and comprehensive system of plans, it also made all development, outside certain categories, subject to specific consent by the local planning authority. The exceptions are types of development which are permitted by a general or specific consent laid down in a statutory instrument, a General Development Order or a Special Development Order; development by the Crown, which is however governed by a system of consultation with the local planning authority, the equivalent in practice of a normal planning procedure; and development by a local authority or statutory undertaker which requires spending authorisation by the government department, such authorisation carrying a 'deemed' planning permission. Development by a local planning authority which accords with its approved development plan is also deemed to have permission. Development which is the subject of a parliamentary bill, for example the present Channel Tunnel proposal, is given planning permission by that enactment. There are special statutory provisions for road developments.

2.22   The meaning of development is carefully defined in the planning laws. It is, in general terms, the carrying out of building, engineering, mining or other operations in, on, over or under land; and the making of any material change in the use of any buildings or land. Many of the terms are given further specific definition, and a number of activities are specifically included within the term development. Other activities are specifically excluded, namely: the use of land, and buildings on it, for agriculture and forestry; improvement, alteration and maintenance which does not materially affect the external appearance of a building; and the use of any building or land within the curtilage of a dwelling house for 'incidental' purposes; work by local authorities and statutory undertakers in connection with the inspection, repair and renewal of sewers, mains, pipes, cables and other apparatus; and road maintenance and repair within the boundaries of the road.

2.23 The 1971 Act says that displaying an advertisement on the external part of a building not normally used for this purpose is a material change of use. Beyond that the term 'material change of use' is not given specific definition in law but it has been defined by the courts as a 'question of fact and degree to be determined in the light of given circumstances'. There is a good deal of case law on the issue. Under a statutory instrument, the Use Classes Order (UCO) (SI 1972, No.1385), many changes of use are exempted from the definition of development. The UCO specifies some 18 different classes of use—such as 'shop', 'office' and 'industrial building'—within which changes of particular use may be made without planning permission.

2.24 Another statutory instrument, the General Development Order (GDO) (SI 1977, No.289, and amendments), itself constitutes the necessary permission for certain types of development. These include certain developments by public authorities and nationalised industries and the limited alteration or enlargement of buildings. The permission given by the order is tightly circumscribed. To clarify the position, a developer can ask the local planning authority to determine whether the action he intends to take constitutes development and if so, whether planning permission is needed. The GDO also lays down the procedures for making and dealing with planning applications.

2.25 Local planning authorities have wide discretion in carrying out their development control responsibilities. Although planning control is one of the purposes for which development plans are made, the authority is required when considering a planning application only to 'have regard' to the provisions of the plan insofar as they are material to the application. The long delays in drawing up and approving development plans have resulted in long periods during which there is no approved development plan in force. They may take any other material considerations into account and can permit a development which is not in accordance with an approved plan. Discretion is circumscribed however by ministerial policies contained in circulars and guidance notes (see Ministry of Housing and Local Government Development Control Policy Notes, 1969, and DOE Circular 1/85), by certain ministerial decisions given on appeal which have a general relevance, and by the rulings of the courts on such questions as what constitutes proper and reasonable considerations. There is a general presumption in favour of permission being given unless there are good planning reasons for refusal. The current government policy set out in DOE Circular 22/80 is that authorities should always grant permission 'having regard to all material considerations, unless there are sound and clear cut reasons for refusal'.

2.26 The local planning authority can allow or deny planning permission or grant it 'subject to such conditions as they think fit'. The authority's discretion to impose conditions is wide but the conditions must relate to planning objectives, not those of other policies. Specifically, the developer can be required to begin, and on service of a notice to complete, operations within a given time; the duration of the permission can be limited; or conditions can be imposed to regulate the development or use of any land under the applicant's control, whether or not it is the land to which the application relates. The authority can negotiate with the developer an agreement regulating or restricting the development and containing 'incidental and consequential provisions', including a financial contribution to the authority. Such 'planning gain' can include the provision by the developer of essential infrastructure which the authority would otherwise have to provide at cost to itself. The question of planning gain is of some moment, since a planning authority might use its power to refuse permission to ask for anything a developer might be willing to pay in order to receive consent. By the same token a developer might offer inducements to a planning authority to overlook good planning reasons against a development. In Circular 22/83 the Department of the Environment stated that a wholly unacceptable development should not be permitted just because of extraneous benefits offered by a developer, and that the authority was not entitled to treat an applicant's need for permission as an opportunity to obtain extraneous benefit or advantage or to exact a payment for the benefit of ratepayers at large. The circular set out tests of reasonableness to be applied by planning authorities in seeking gain.

2.27 Development control policies cover a wide range of issues: from the type of development (that is, residential, commercial, industrial etc) appropriate to particular areas through questions of density; access; traffic generation; layout and landscaping of sites; and the height, elevation, and design of buildings and materials used. Generally speaking, more stringent policies are applied in areas designated for special protection, that is, national parks and areas of outstanding natural beauty, countryside and urban conservation areas, and green belts.

2.28 A developer may seek an outline planning permission which the authority may give subject to its subsequent approval of any 'reserved' matters such as the siting and design of buildings. The authority may however refuse to consider the application unless further details are provided. A permission once given may be revoked or modified by the authority before a change of use takes place or a development is completed, in which case compensation is payable. Any development or use whether specifically permitted or established before the introduction of development control can be stopped on planning grounds by a discontinuance order, and again compensation is payable. Development or change of use undertaken without planning permission can be stopped by an enforcement notice specifying the action to be taken. Ignoring the notice renders the developer liable on conviction to a fine and a daily penalty until the notice is obeyed. Authorities are not obliged to issue enforcement notices on breaches of development control and can only do so on planning grounds.

2.29 The number of planning applications made each year has tended to vary within a range of 400,000 to 600,000 (in England and Wales). The figures for England in 1984/5 were 421,000 received, 399,000 determined, and 345,000 (86 per cent) granted. Following a rapid increase in applications from 425,000 to 615,000 between 1968 and 1972, and growing delays in their determination, an official review of the development control system was carried out by George Dobry QC (Review of Development Control System: Final Report. HMSO 1975). By the time he reported, however, the situation had changed and most of his specific recommendations for improving and expediting the process were not acted upon. The question of delay was also examined in 1976-77 by the Commons Expenditure Committee (Eighth Report of the Expenditure Committee from the Sessions 1976/77: Planning Procedures. House of Commons Papers 395. HMSO 1977). In 1979 the Thatcher government required local planning authorities to make quarterly statistical returns, including the time taken to determine applications.

43

The present position

2.30   The present government has sought to lessen the scope of planning control and to reduce delays. The 1980 Local Government, Planning and Land Act gave power to establish Enterprise Zones where a general planning permission exists for development which falls within parameters established by the local planning authority in drawing up the Enterprise Zones scheme. Similar rules will apply in Simplified Planning Zones proposed in the current Housing and Planning Bill. Department of the Environment Circular 22/80, noted above, which called for a more positive attitude towards development and speedier processing of applications, was followed by similar references to development control in subsequent circulars. Circular 14/85 which accompanied the government white paper 'Lifting the Burden' went further in saying there should always be a presumption in favour of development unless it would 'cause demonstrable harm to interests of acknowledged importance'. The Circular was regarded by some as a marked downgrading of development plans which, it said, should not be seen as overriding other material considerations. It said that reasons for refusing planning consent must always be 'precise, specific and relevant' and that planning authorities should avoid 'unnecessarily onerous and complex controls'. Under an EEC Directive promulgated in 1985, major development proposals likely to have a significant effect on the environment by virtue of their nature, size or location will have to be accompanied by an Environmental Impact Assessment (EIA). The preparation of such reports has already been adopted informally in some quarters, notably the oil industry, and EIAs have been prepared for some recent major schemes including the Channel Tunnel and the Dounreay plutonium reprocessing plant. In April 1986 the Department of the Environment announced proposals for implementing the Directive by requiring EIAs to be submitted with planning applications for schemes on the Directive's mandatory list which includes oil refineries, asbestos works, and integrated steel and chemical works. Mandatory list developments not subject to town and country planning legislation, including power stations, motorways and ports, would be subjected to the 'same broad principles'. The Secretary of State for the Environment would reserve powers to direct that EIAs be prepared for schemes on the Directive's much longer secondary list and local planning authorities could seek voluntary submission of EIAs on such schemes, the Department said, pointing out that environmental effects were among the material considerations local planning authorities must take into account in considering an application.

Appeals and inquiries

2.31 Any applicant for planning permission aggrieved by the local planning authority's refusal or imposition of conditions can appeal to the planning minister. Appeals may also be made against an authority's failure to determine an application within the statutory period of eight weeks, against enforcement notices, and on a number of other specific actions taken by or permissions refused by a local planning authority. In determining the appeal, the minister, or an inspector acting in his name, can reverse the authority's decision, quash, moderate or strengthen conditions imposed by the authority, or act as if the application had been made to him in the first place. The minister's decision, like that of a local planning authority, is a matter of judgement. He is not required, for example, to act in accordance with an approved structure plan or adopted local plan. He is however obliged to act reasonably, and although his decision is final it may be challenged in the courts on a point of law, the 'reasonableness of the decision'.

2.32 Either the applicant or the authority can demand to be heard in private by an inspector before the appeal is determined. Public inquiries into appeals are held at the discretion of the minister or the inspector planning the appeal, except that an inspector can be directed by the minister to hold an inquiry. There is no right of appeal by a third party against a planning decision but the holding of an inquiry allows objectors and supporters of a proposal to have their views heard and considered. Many appeals are withdrawn before determination—the proportion has fallen from about 30 per cent to 20 per cent over the last decade. The majority of those that go forward, between 70 and 80 per cent, are determined on the basis of written representations. Under the 1968 Act certain appeals could be heard and determined by an inspector. Under 1981 regulations (SI 1981, No. 804), all planning applications and enforcement appeals were transferred to the inspectorate, although the minister can retrieve responsibility on specific cases. The inspectorate is a body of full time and part time staff employed by the Department of the Environment. Most, but not all, are chartered town planners or members of associated professions. The minister can also call on the services of others, often planners or lawyers, to act as inspectors and this is done most particularly in the case of major inquiries.

2.33 The number of appeals varies between about 11,000 and 17,000 a year. The number received in 1985 (17,053) was the largest since 1973 and the number determined that year (14,639) was a record. The proportion succeeding, while variable, has increased over the past decade from about 25 per cent to 41 per cent. The proportion of written representation appeals determined by the minister fell from 20.7 per cent to 3.1 per cent between 1972 and 1983, and that of inquiries from 47.2 per cent to 20.2 per cent. About half of all appeals relate to land at or near the home of the appellant.

2.34   The minister has power to call in and determine himself any planning application, and certain types of application must be notified to him so that he can consider so doing. Very few applications are called in. They are usually cases in which national policy or interest or difficult technical issues are involved, or to which more than local objection is taken. When an application is called in either the applicant or the planning authority can demand a public inquiry.

2.35   The procedure for public inquiries is laid down in rules (SO 1974, No.419) covering such matters as the notification of parties, the fixing of the time, date and place of the inquiry, the submission of written statements and documents, the rights of representation and attendance, and site inspections. Most emanate from the 1957 report of the Franks Committee on Administrative Tribunals and Inquiries (Cmnd No.218, HMSO 1957), which formalised the procedure and gave emphasis to judicial aspects. The inspector's decision must be given in writing, together with reasons supporting it. When the minister determines an appeal or application, he is not obliged to uphold the decision of the inspector.

2.36   Non statutory public inquiries are held by ministers on developments which require their authorisation, by which the development receives 'deemed' planning permission. These include developments by government departments, statutory undertakers and local authorities.

2.37   Powers which have never been used exist under the 1968 and 1971 Town and Country Planning Acts to substitute for a normal public inquiry a Planning Inquiry Commission, comprising a chairman and two to four other members, with the duty of carrying out detailed investigations as well as hearing evidence. The procedure is intended for developments raising issues of national or regional importance or presenting unfamiliar technical or scientific aspects. It is a two stage process, the second step consisting of a local planning inquiry.

Consultation and participation

2.38   Local planning authorities are required by law to allow the general public to participate in plan making, to consult certain bodies, and to publicise and consider representations on certain planning applications. Beyond the minimum statutory requirements, the scope of consultation and participation as set out in ministerial circulars and guidance notes tends to be vague and ambiguous, resulting in wide variations in practice and uncertainty among the public about the extent of its rights.

2.39 The right of participation in plan making was introduced by the 1968 Town and Country Planning Act. Proposals of a rather general nature for securing public participation were made in the Skeffington Report (Report of the Committee on Public Participation in Planning: People and Planning. HMSO 1969), published the following year. Its two positive recommendations, the appointment of community development officers to help citizens take part in planning and community forums for the discussion of planning issues, have never been put into effect.

2.40 The present government has somewhat reduced the formal public participation requirements in the interests of speedier planning, while encouraging consultation with developers. Under the 1980 Local Government, Planning and Land Act county planning authorities are required when preparing structure plans to give adequate publicity to the matters they propose to include, to give those interested an adequate opportunity to make representations, and to consider such representations. They are required to consult district planning authorities and are asked to consult government departments and other public bodies likely to be affected. They are also asked to discuss with house builders the provision of a five year supply of land. The planning minister is required to consider all objections and representations on a published draft structure plan and can allow discussion on issues he selects at an examination in public. Prior to the 1980 Act an examination in public was mandatory but this is no longer the case in respect of revised plans. There are similar provisions for local plans.

2.41 Planning authorities are required to give publicity to development proposals affecting the appearance of a conservation area or listed building; to specified 'bad neighbour' developments like public conveniences, mineral workings, tall buildings etc; and developments which substantially and materially differ from development plan provisions. These amount to about 10 per cent of planning applications. Publicity for other types of development is generally at the discretion of the planning authority. District planning authorities are required to notify county authorities of applications which relate to county matters, and parish councils can require planning authorities to inform them of applications relating to their area.

Land values, compensation and fees

2.42 Town and country planning is an intervention in the market which affects the value of land and other property. Prewar planning was hindered by the requirement that planning authorities pay compensation to owners denied the right to develop their land. But when planning authorities allow development to take place they also create an increase or betterment in the value of land which arguably should belong to the community rather than the individual owner who has himself done nothing to bring about the increase in value. By the same token public authorities should be able to acquire land for public development without paying for the extra value that development has brought about.

2.43 These questions raise complex problems which the 1947 Act attempted to resolve by effectively nationalising development rights and values. Since then, no compensation has been payable, except in a few special cases, when planning permission is refused. Special interim arrangements were made for compensating those who could claim their land had a development value at the time the Act came into force. Any increase in value created by a planning permission became subject to a 100 per cent development charge. The scheme caused many difficulties in practice and in 1954 the development charge was abandoned. In 1959 'fair market value' was restored as the basis of compensation for land compulsorily purchased for public development. There have been a variety of attempts since then to deal with the betterment question by levies and taxes. The latest of these, the development land tax, was abandoned in 1985.

2.44 Compensation is payable by a local planning authority in certain circumstances in which it refuses permission for new development, revokes or modifies or removes an existing planning permission, or imposes conditions. In certain circumstances a planning authority can be required to buy land on which it has refused planning permission or imposed conditions on development. House owners and owner-occupiers of farms and small businesses can also require their property to be purchased if it is 'blighted', that is, its resale value is diminished, by certain structure and development plan provisions or public sector development intentions, including road building.

2.45 The 1980 Local Government, Planning and Land Act introduced fees for planning applications. The present rates prescribed by government start at £12, £24 and £47 per unit according to the type of development (for example, £47 per house created) and are subject to maximum limits.

Planning authorities and agencies

Central government

2.46 The establishment of a central government department for land use planning was the first step in creating the modern planning system. Responsibility had previously rested with the Minister of Health. In 1943 the Minister of Town and Country Planning Act created a new minister and a new ministry, whose titles were changed in 1951 first to Local Government and Planning, then to Housing and Local Government. A short-lived office of Secretary of State for Local Government and Regional Planning established in 1969 to oversee the transport and the housing and local government ministries paved the way for the creation in 1970 of the Department of the Environment, drawing together responsibility for housing, local government, planning, transport and environmental conservation and protection. Transport is now once again a separate department.

2.47 The planning minister is charged with 'securing consistency and continuity in the framing and execution of a national policy with respect to the use and development of land'. The minister is, of course, responsible within government and through Parliament for framing new legislation, making regulations, rules and orders under existing legislation, and enunciating policy in the form of statements, circulars and decisions. His role in relation to development plans, development control and appeals has been described above. It is only necessary perhaps to stress that he has considerable reserve power to direct local planning authorities to carry out their functions or, in default, to exercise those functions himself. As housing minister he also exercises responsibility for what has been throughout most of the post war period one of the major development activities affecting planning. He is additionally the sponsoring minister for the construction industry generally. He is responsible for listing ancient monuments and buildings of special historical or architectural interest, and for the work of development agencies, the Countryside Commission and the Nature Conservancy Council.

2.48 Although most departments of state have a profound influence on social and economic factors affecting town and country planning, and many are significant land users, there is no central machinery for coordinating their activities in this respect. There

49

has at times been some regional coordination through joint committees or boards of civil servants.

Local government

2.49 The 1947 Act gave responsibility for town and country planning to counties and county boroughs, that is to a single authority within each major local government area. In the counties development control could be, and increasingly was, delegated to lower tier district councils. Although the 1968 Act structure planning system was designed for all purpose unitary authorities the 1974 local government reorganisation redistributed planning functions, making the upper tier counties responsible for structure planning, for agreeing with districts a scheme of local plan making and development control policy, and for determining planning applications of strategic significance. The preparation of most local plans and the exercise of day to day development control was allocated to the lower tier of district authorities, closer to the ground. Districts were required however to inform counties of applications which might substantially affect county interests, and could be directed by the county to refuse such applications. The 1980 Local Government, Planning and Land Act shifted the balance in favour of district councils by making them responsible for determining all planning applications formerly classified as county matters except those relating to mineral and related workings and to national parks. The development control scheme was largely superceded by arrangements for consultation between the two levels.

2.50 Local authorities also have specific powers to acquire land, if necessary by compulsory purchase, for planning purposes, including comprehensive redevelopment, and to sell land for development. Under the 1975 Community Land Act, repealed by the 1980 Act, local authorities were given stronger powers for compulsory purchase of land to control development in accordance with the needs and priorities of the community, and to restore to the community the increase in value of land resulting from its efforts.

2.51 In London, where local government was reorganised a decade earlier, the division of planning responsibilities between the Greater London Council (GLC) and the boroughs was similar to that adopted elsewhere but rather more complex and governed by special procedures in the 1971 Act. The GLC was responsible for preparing a strategic, later redesignated structure, plan and was the local planning authority for certain areas and developments of strategic importance. The boroughs were responsible for local plan making and development control.

2.52   With the demise of the GLC, borough councils are required to prepare 'unitary' plans. They are to be in two parts, the first a written statement of the authority's general policies for development and land use, the second a written statement of policies and proposals supported by a map and a reasoned justification. The second part will embrace already adopted local plans. The same arrangements apply in the six English metropolitan areas whose county councils have also been abolished. In each of these areas the regional offices of the Department of the Environment are to issue strategic guidance to the boroughs. Greater London has a statutory joint committee of borough representatives, the London Planning Advisory Committee. It is to advise the boroughs (and the DOE) on matters of common interest relating to planning and development and has a small planning staff. The Association of London Authorities, a grouping of Labour controlled boroughs, has set up its own rather larger planning unit to advise on London-wide issues. The other metropolitan areas do not have statutory joint bodies but in most of them the districts have made a variety of arrangements for coordination of planning research and information and other planning and development related activities.

Development corporations

2.53   The creation of new towns, a fundamental aspect of the consensus on post war planning and redevelopment, was allocated on the recommendation of a committee chaired by Lord Reith to ad hoc agencies responsible to Parliament. The 1946 New Towns Act accordingly allowed the planning minister to designate new town areas and appoint development corporations. The Act empowered the corporations to acquire, hold, manage and dispose of land and other property, to provide services, carry out any business or undertaking in or for the purpose of the new town, and generally to do anything else 'necessary or expedient for the purposes of the new town'. Development corporations are financed by the Treasury. Their planning and development activities are subject to approval by the planning minister and do not come under the control of the local planning authority. The 1959 New Towns Act established the Commission for New Towns to take over the assets and management of mature new towns. Under the New Towns (Amendment) Act 1976 housing and related assets of the new towns in England and Wales were transfered to local authorities. The new town programme in England and Wales is now being wound up, and the assets sold to the private sector. The Scottish new town development corporations, however, are to remain in being.

2.54   The 1980 Local Government, Planning and Land Act empowered the minister to designate urban development areas and
establish urban development corporations within Greater London
and the six English metropolitan counties. The corporations have
similar powers to the new town development corporations. Their
purpose is to regenerate the designated area by bringing land and
buildings into effective use, encouraging the development of new
industry and commerce, creating an attractive environment and
ensuring that housing and social facilities are available to
encourage people to live and work in the area. By ministerial order,
an urban development corporation can become the local planning
authority for all or part of its area. New town and urban
development corporations may also draw up Enterprise Zone
schemes and become the planning authority for the zone.

Countryside Commission

2.55   The Countryside Commission, created in 1968, is the suc-
cessor to the National Parks Commission established by the
National Parks and Access to the Countryside Act 1949. It is
responsible for designating national parks, areas of outstanding
natural beauty, long distance footpaths and heritage coasts and for
giving advice on their planning, management and administration. It
has a general duty of advising ministers and public bodies on all
matters relating to the countryside. It is also the Commission's duty
to assist and promote the provision of facilities for the enjoyment of
the countryside, to conserve and enhance the natural beauty and
amenity of the countryside and to secure public access. It can grant
aid to local initiatives to conserve and improve the countryside.

Nature Conservancy Council

2.56   The Nature Conservancy Council, constituted by Royal
Charter in 1949, is charged with establishing and managing nature
reserves and has powers to acquire land or make agreements with
landowners for this purpose. It is also responsible for identifying
and protecting geological and biological sites of special scientific
interest. Under the 1981 Wildlife and Countryside Act it is required
to renotify local planning authorities, the government and landowners of sites of special scientific interest (SSSIs) originally
designated under the 1949 National Parks Act as well as notifying
them of new sites, a process still in train. The Council is obliged to
make for each SSSI a list of potentially damaging operations which
may only be carried out with its authority, and can make
agreements, including payment to owners, for the management of
the land. It has a duty to advise the government on biological and

geological matters, including the impact on these interests of major development schemes, and to further nature conservation generally.

Scotland

2.57 Responsibility in Scotland for town and country planning, and many contingent matters, is vested in the Scottish Secretary of State. The planning system, although generally similar to that in England and Wales, has a number of significant differences.

2.58 The 1973 Local Government (Scotland) Act created a two tier system of regional and district councils plus three single tier island area authorities. In six regions the regional authority is responsible for structure plans and the district for local plans. In the three less populous regions the regional authority has all planning functions. They and the three island authorities are 'general planning authorities'. Regional and general planning authorities must prepare structure plans for each cohesive part of their areas, but the plans need not cover every part of the region.

2.59 Structure planning has been supplemented by the introduction of the 'regional report' (Scottish Development Department, Circular 4/1975), which has several functions. It provides the basis for discussion between the Secretary of State and the region about general development policy, and guidance for the preparation or review of structure plans, while in the absence of structure plans it serves as a guide to development control. The report, which may cover the whole or part of a region, must be based on a survey and consultation with affected local authorities and must be submitted to the Secretary of State and published with his observations. No formal approval or adoption is required. Planning authorities must take account of the report and the Secretary of State's observations.

2.60 General and district planning authorities must prepare local plans for all parts of their district. Districts must obtain the consent of the regional authority to prepare a local plan if a structure plan or regional report which would have a significant impact on the local plan area is under preparation. Local plans need only the approval of the responsible authority to bring them into operation. They may however be called in either by the Secretary of State or the regional authority.

2.61 Development control is the responsibility of district and general planning authorities. Regional authorities may call in applications when the development does not conform to an approved structure plan or raises a new planning issue of general significance to the district. The Secretary of State also has call in powers. Regional authorities must be informed of proposals to modify, revoke or discontinue planning permissions and have default powers to make such orders themselves. There is a right of appeal to the Secretary of State in all cases.

2.62   Scotland has also developed a unique system of National Planning Guidelines (see SDD Circular 19/1977), born out of a 1972 Select Committee recommendation (Select Committee on Land Resource Use in Scotland) that the government should draw up a structure plan for the whole country. There are currently six sets of guidelines dealing with coastal planning for North Sea oil and gas, aggregate workings, major shopping developments, priorities for development planning, skiing developments, and high technology industry. The guidelines define the national interest in the way land is used and what should be done to safeguard or promote that interest, indicate zones in which development is to be preferred or resisted, and give advance warning of issues on which the Secretary of State may call in applications. They are accompanied by a series of land use summary sheets derived from the resource surveys on which the guidelines are based. The guidelines are being incorporated into regional reports and development plans.

2.63   Scotland has two special government-appointed agencies to foster and aid development, the Highlands and Islands Development Board and the Scottish Development Agency (SDA). The SDA, which has land acquisition and grant-making powers, plays a prominant role in collaboration with other agencies and authorities in urban regeneration schemes. It is also responsible for derelict land reclamation. There is a separate Countryside Commission for Scotland.

Wales

2.64   Central responsibility for planning is vested in the Secretary of State for Wales. The planning system is generally the same as in England. There is a Land Authority which retains powers of land acquisition and disposal created by the Community Land Act and expunged elsewhere by the 1980 Local Government, Planning and Land Act. It buys land and makes it available for sale and development by providing infrastructure and obtaining planning permission. Most is destined for house building. There is also a Welsh Development Agency with similar powers to the SDA.

PART II OPINION

Chapter 3 Why Have Planning At All?

3.1 We have not found either in the evidence given to us in the course of the Inquiry or elsewhere any serious dissent from the bedrock principle on which planning has been based since 1947: namely that no change should be made in the use to which land is put without the prior permission of a public authority. The general acceptance of this principle is fundamental: it involves at least that there must be definitions of what constitutes a development, authorities empowered to consider applications and to grant or refuse permissions, rules of procedure and where possible policies of substance to enable applicants to know where they stand, and means to resolve disputes or to hear appeals from the decisions of those authorities. So much appears to be common ground. But beyond this point agreement ends: the consensus on the purposes and aims of planning which seemed assured in the glad confident morning of 1947 has vanished like the dew.

3.2 We did not originally address the question, 'Why have planning at all?' to those whom we consulted. But it has become clear that disagreement about the reasons for planning underlie many of the other differences of view which we shall analyse and explore below.

3.3 Acceptance of the fundamental principle appears to be based on two propositions: a common recognition of land as a unique resource—it is for example inherently subject to neighbourhood effects in a way that other resources are not—and the central importance of environmental controls in creating and conserving acceptable living conditions. Particular care has to be taken to ensure that land is used both efficiently and effectively and that long term interests are not sacrificed for short term advantage (Bancroft, Burns, Donnison, Wibberley, LBA, RIBA). [The names and initials in brackets in this and the following chapters refer to the evidence submitted to the Inquiry by the people and organisations whose full names are listed in Appendix II.] There is an inherent public interest in all decisions about development (Cherry, CPRE, CSLA, Crowther, RTPI, Coppock), and it is necessary that the 'social costs' of any development should be taken into account before it goes ahead (RTPI, CPOS). It is, moreover, generally desirable that decisions on changes of land use should be coordinated with the allocation of other resources, such as transport, schools, social services and so forth (Bor, Hall D, CSLA, Burns, Buchanan, RTPI, Hart District Council). So much at least is desirable to avoid waste and confusion and to prevent the short term exploitation of the land to the detriment of the long term interests of the community.

3.4 Many however go beyond this basic view of planning as damage limitation and see it as a necessary, positive force for the creation of a satisfactory physical environment (Bancroft, Burns, Cherry, Gibberd, RIBA, RTPI, Doubleday, LDEC, Thorburn). And some go further in stressing the importance of planning for conserving and creating 'communities' with a quality of life sustained by access to a full and balanced range of services, facilities and opportunities for work and leisure (CLA, Buchanan, RTPI, Hart District Council). There is strong support too for encouraging the variety and richness of environments, both social and physical, and for ensuring that all urban environments are human in scale and identity (Cherry, Allison, Ravetz, Ward). More broadly yet some argue that planning is needed so that all communities can release their full potential for economic and social development, and to ensure a rational distribution of population, employment and recreation across the whole nation (Buchanan). And finally there is some support for planning as an instrument for the redistribution of wealth, so that in the interests of social justice land is allocated according to the needs rather than the means of the people (Eversley, RIG, Hart District Council).

3.5 Town and country planning is therefore required to tackle any impediments to the achievement of these broad aspirations: it must assist to contain urban sprawl and to reduce congestion (LGBC, CPRE, Hart District Council, Gibberd, Thomas), to improve the housing stock (CPRE, RTPI), to reclaim derelict land (Higgins, CPRE), to prevent the despoliation of the countryside (Buchanan, Wibberley, Devon Conservation Forum), the contamination of the environment, and the over exploitation of natural resources (Allison, Ravetz, RTPI), to revive the inner cities (CPRE, CLA, Denman, Bor, Allison, Devon Conservation Forum), to encourage rebuilding (CSLA, LBA, Thorburn), and to ensure that our communities develop as their citizens wish (CLA, Wilmott, Hall D, Cherry). To achieve all of this planning should be part and parcel of a broader, publicly accountable (Friend, Hall D, McConnell) process of social, environmental and economic planning—physical or land use planning must not be viewed in isolation from other forms of public sector activity (Bancroft, Higgins, RTPI, Bor, RIG). Indeed some of the evidence we have heard argues that planning should take on a leading role in encouraging the development of a wider planning function (RTPI, McConnell).

3.6   It is hardly surprising that this ambitious role for planning is questioned and indeed rejected by others, who do not see 'planned' intervention by government in the process of development as the answer to our problems and warn against shackling self help, individual initiative and private enterprise (Ward, ARC, Denman, CBI). The familiar complaint arising from the practical experience of the development industry reflects a much wider scepticism if not about the desirability of an ambitious role for planning then about its feasibility. For planning in general has been subjected to formidable criticism which ranges from high theory to low practice. There is first the fundamental philosophical attack on government intervention in economic affairs seen in its most sophisticated and developed form in the work of F A von Hayek.[1] Then there is the similar but more limited critique which draws attention to the costs of government intervention.[2] And last but not least are the criticisms of planning that arise from observation and experience of its failures in practice: the theme of planning disasters, great and small, which arise from some combination of hubris, intellectual confusion and the inexorable operation of Murphy's Law.[3] One does not have to accept Hayek's equation of the market economy with prosperity, the rule of law and liberty, in order to see the force of his argument that a central authority cannot command the information which would be necessary for it to substitute its judgement for the' dispersed information and preferences of a multitude of firms and individuals. The second line of criticism does not deny that intervention may be effective, but demands that the costs of intervention be properly taken into account in assessing its desirability. The third argument reflects both disappointment with the results of planning, physical, economic and social, and an analysis of the institutional factors which frustrate rationalistic expectations of policy making. To put the matter crudely the potential planner has to ask himself how he knows where he wants to intervene and how much it will cost to do so, and whether the instruments at his disposal will produce the results he intends.

3.7   It cannot be said that the arguments in favour of land use planning which we have encountered address themselves directly to these questions. We may however observe of these general criticisms that planning is not necessarily and has not in fact been a centralised system of decision making; that despite its costs it is extensively practised in the great corporations, private as well as public, which are the most successful and characteristic organisations of modern times; and that against its failures are many successes which do not attract as much attention. And if we reverse the presumptions we can make a case for planning from the observations made to us about the failings of private decisions on land use through the market (MPOS). The question then becomes under what circumstances a planned system of change in land use can overcome those failings without itself adding yet greater problems. Differences of interest, value and judgement will remain as to the necessity of intervention, the costs of intervention and the balance of advantage, public and private, arising from intervention. But the nature of the differences will, we hope, stand more clearly revealeᴏ.

3.8   Markets work as well as they do because they operate on the basis of voluntary trade or exchange. Each party to an exchange has something to gain. On the one hand the producer sells a good or service at a price which both covers his costs and provides him with an element of profit. On the other hand the consumer buys something which he in turn wants. The value of the good he buys is at least as great to him as the money (or other goods and services) he foregoes in return.

3.9   Despite these advantages a number of problems arise in this exchange relationship. In the evidence presented to us, we have found little disagreement about the disadvantages of an unfettered private development system: disagreement relates mainly to the costs of the means adopted to deal with them.

Sources of failure in the private development process

Neighbourhood effects
3.10   The main difficulty is that firms and households, in building and in making land use changes, often impose 'costs' on others, for which they do not have to pay. These 'external costs' or 'neighbourhood effects' may lead to actual losses of money or amenity or may impose some extra burden on those receiving them. As a result they may be considered unfair or even lead to inefficiencies in the way society's scarce resources are used— especially if their effect is large enough.

3.11   Examples cited in evidence to us include the control of nuisances and of blight from development (Bor, Hall D, LBA), the prevention of injury and pollution (ARC, Allison, Burns, Thomas, EHO), checks on the environmental impact of development (Hall D, NCC, CSLA), and or hazardous materials associated with development (Ravetz), the prevention of waste (Ravetz), and of the destruction of human scale and identity in the environment (Cherry), and the recovery of the social costs of development (MPOS).

Public goods

3.12 A second source of private system 'failure' concerns its inability to provide types of buildings and land use which possess the characteristics of 'public goods'. In the private system firms and households fail to make certain types of land use or building change even though their total (social and private) benefits exceed their costs. One of the main reasons for this is the difficulty, in many instances, of recovering the costs of making these changes from the prices that can be charged—usually because it is too costly or impracticable to exclude, from the benefits of the land use or building, anyone who does not pay something towards the cost of providing those benefits.

3.13 Among the arguments for planning intervention here are the encouragement of public benefits from development (LBA, Allison, RTPI), the efficient provision of land for essential infrastructure like schools (Bancroft, Cherry), access to open space (Buchanan, Bor, Wibberley) and an economic transport system (Buchanan), a contribution from developers to the maintenance and replacement of the infrastructure (CPRE, Hart District Council) and the protection of the countryside (Ramblers Association, CPRE).

Conservation

3.14 A related problem in this respect is that land uses and buildings which have certain 'public good' characteristics and have been produced in the past are in danger of being *destroyed* by the operation of the private development system. For example, natural amenities like clean air *not* produced by the private market at all, or open countryside (very largely the accidental by-product of many unrelated decisions by individual farmers) may well be lost or impaired if private firms find it difficult to 'market' them. A new housing development on a greenfield site, for example, may ruin the amenity or enjoyment people obtain from an expanse of open countryside and yet it may be extremely difficult for those who suffer the 'loss' to express it—they can't buy the view in the market place to keep it for themselves.

59

3.15 For these reasons conservation of many different types of 'resource' is not something the private development system takes sufficiently seriously. Resources which are said to require protection include flora, fauna, places of outstanding natural beauty and scientific interest (Bancroft), the character and identity of communities (Hart District Council), agricultural land (Buchanan, Burns, Thorburn, Allison), lowland countryside (Buchanan, CPRE), the built and natural heritage (Burns, CSLA, Buchanan, Thorburn, LGBC), natural resources, including energy, water, the atmosphere (Ravetz, Thomas, Thorburn), rural amenities (CPRE), especially informal amenities for recreation (CLA), and wildlife on farmland (Wibberley). These are all aspects of a general argument that development must be compatible with conservation (Cherry, Allison, Buchanan, RIBA).

The power of monopoly and economies of large scale development
3.16 In the private system firms often secure some degree of monopolistic power over the market they are supplying, with a number of consequences. First of all there is the tendency to stifle innovation—it is the knowledge and pressure of competition which most often forces firms to supply products which better or more cheaply satisfy consumer wants. Secondly monopolistic power can mean higher prices for consumers. The problem of monopoly is of course a general one, not necessarily related to land use, and indeed other anti-monopoly policies can be and are used. Some sources of monopoly are however directly related to land use, so that planning may prove the best way of dealing with them.

3.17 A common example of monopoly in action is the superstore or hypermarket. A town is served by a range of small shopkeepers and their shops—there is competition between grocers, chemists, furniture shops, small supermarkets and so forth—and then a superstore proposal is made. The new shop sells a large number of product ranges under one roof, has excellent car parking facilities and is owned by a single proprietor. Because of bulk purchasing and handling the superstore can sell virtually all of its goods at a lower price than existing traders. For the consumer this seems a good deal. But if the new superstore is able to capture a large part of the existing shops' demand then their profits and thus existence may be threatened. With their demise the superstore may then increase its prices again. With little risk of competition, prices can then be higher than they were before the superstore.

3.18 A second example where monopolistic power can be important is when a development project requires the assembly of a large site which is currently split up amongst many different small scale landowners. The private developer can find that the owner of the very last plot required will attempt to bid up the price of his property, and see his profits (and incentive to develop) considerably impaired. In such circumstances an organisation with rights of compulsion over the landowner who is 'holding-out' may be required to resolve the issue.

3.19 There are however occasions when it may be expedient to encourage the circumstances which help to produce monopolies in the first place. The provision of a drainage system, a system of water supply, and a public transport network, for example, tends to work out much cheaper when *one* organisation provides them all. If it then acts in typically monopolistic fashion the benefits for the public may be cancelled out. The essential point in all this is the importance of a public decision on the merits of a monopoly in any particular situation.

Distribution and equality
3.20 In the private system some individuals and households, especially those with low incomes, little accumulated wealth or special needs, are often poorly served by the market. The distribution of goods and services generated by the market is heavily influenced by the initial endowment of resources—land, labour and capital—which people and organisations bring to the market. The rich can afford the best the market can supply. The poor are left with the worst, which at times means nothing at all. And when this applies to basic goods like dwellings and open space the heavy penalties that may be imposed on the poor are obvious. As with monopoly, governments have instruments at their disposal unconnected with land use, but there are certain sources of inequality that planning may be particularly suited for dealing with.

3.21 Apart from the argument that some part of profit from development should accrue to the community as a whole (Bor, Hall D, Eversley, RTPI, LBA), there is seen to be a case for redistribution to benefit the disadvantaged (Bor, Ravetz, Buchanan) through the provision of employment and housing in poor areas (Eversley), to improve the quality of life in the inner cities (Bor, Haar), to achieve national minimum standards for the provision of housing, jobs, schools, recreation and transport (Doubleday, Buchanan, RTPI, Hart District Council), and to maintain a regional balance of population, employment and wealth (Buchanan, Hart District Council); there is a need to protect minorities (Haar), and to direct development to areas needing development (CSLA).

61

Community and unethical behaviour by market participants
3.22 The fundamental argument for the free market, ever since Adam Smith, has been the contention that individuals, in selfish pursuit of their own goals, help to produce outcomes which are good for society as a whole. However, such behaviour is not always to be considered desirable. There are many instances relevant to land use where the pursuit of individual interest produces outcomes or actions which may be socially unacceptable. We have already noted the importance of neighbourhood effects but behaviour and its outcomes may also be considered unacceptable on quasi-moral or ethical grounds—the production of slum housing, and of betting or sex shops are good examples. Most families and individuals for example may well prefer (and thus the 'market' may provide) homogeneous neighbourhoods rather than neighbourhoods diversified with respect to incomes, social class, ages and stages in the life cycle of the individuals who compose them. But the advantages associated with mixed or balanced neighbourhood communities have long been advocated—the reduction of social and racial tensions, a more equitable spread of schools, social facilities and, importantly, of tax burdens, and the complementarity of communities made up of people of different ages and lifestyles. 'Market choices over location seem excessively geared towards the preferences of the "dominant consumer"—typically pictured as the male head of household with a good income and two cars. The needs of less powerful consumers—such as old people, working wives and perhaps teenagers—deserve more attention'[5] than the market takes into account. Indeed there is plenty of evidence that the market may well operate to destroy more communal patterns of living— where communities get in the way of profitable property development. The need to sustain and develop communities is certainly thought to be a ground for planning intervention (CSLA, Allison, Donnison, Hart District Council).

Unemployment and slow economic growth
3.23 It is sometimes argued that the unfettered operation of a free market can lead to slow economic growth and to unemployment. Explanations of these problems include cyclical deficiencies in the aggregate demand for goods and services (including development), structural mismatches between the skills of workers in the economy (and especially the local economies of particular areas) and the type of labour that is demanded by producers, and frictions in the economy which slow down the adjustments workers and firms make to changes in demand, prices and costs.

3.24   Each of these potential causes of macro-economic problems can have links with changes in land use and development. Disincentives to develop, for example, reduce aggregate demand. Where local communities are dominated by industries suffering from long term decline local residents are available for work but their skills do not fit the job openings provided by local patterns of land use. Slow adjustments in the provision of services such as energy or transport infrastructure necessary for the functioning of industry can delay the expansion of the local and the national economy.

3.25   Planning is seen as relevant to the promotion of national economic development (Burns, Allison, RTPI, Thorburn), to tackling regional disparities in employment (Crowther, Eversley, RTPI) and the local problems of inner cities (Haar, Eversley, Bor, Buchanan, RTPI, Storm, Donnison), and to the stimulation of appropriate economic activity in rural areas (CLA, CPRE, Coppock).

What can planning do about it?

3.26   The fact that we can identify weaknesses in the market is not of itself an argument for planning. As a recent review of the pros and cons put it: 'Informed critiques of planning are not made in ignorance of the theoretical limitations of markets, but in the belief that, despite these limitations, markets are still more effective than attempts at central coordination by government'.[6] In recent debate the burden of proof has shifted from showing that markets don't work to showing that planning can work any better. And that means not only better than the market but better than other forms of government intervention, such as taxation, regulation, performance standards or licensing. On the basis of the evidence we have received we think it would be safer to conclude that many experienced people think that planning should be able to make good the deficiencies of the market than that it does so. But in drawing up a balance sheet against which to judge what are reasonable expectations for the future, we have also to acknowledge that it is not planning in general which has to be examined but the British town and country planning system, warts and all. As the comments in the next two chapters will show, many of the failures of planning are attributed to inadequate powers and unsuitable structures rather than weaknesses inherent in the idea of planning itself. There is a second consideration: planning is not simply concerned with the problems created by private decisions on land use. Many of the most important decisions about land use are made in the public sector and the public sector is no more of a monolith or coherent hierarchy than the private sector. It consists of a variety of agencies with their own powers, resources and agenda, loosely connected through the links between their parent departments in central government, and the whole held together by the uncertain disciplines for the control of public expenditure. The job of planning authorities has been to make what sense they could of the local impact of the activities (plans) of these quasi-autonomous public bodies, over whom they enjoy fewer powers than over the private sector. Suffice it to say here that to many of the proponents of planning, and to ourselves, this aspect of the 'system' looms large and it has to be borne continuously in mind in assessing the effectiveness of planning. Planning as we are considering it is a limited part of public sector activity and not to be confused with the whole or to be burdened with its sins. It should therefore come as no surprise if we conclude that on several of the issues listed above planning as such has had relatively little effect one way or the other. Planning has commanded neither the powers nor the authority to influence decisively the pattern of economic change, or the distribution of wealth. Its social prescriptions have been ignored by those who had any choice in the matter and public monopolies have paid no more attention than suburban commuters to the case for balanced communities. By contrast planning has been increasingly successful in the cause of conservation, in the protection and provision of public goods, in the control of private activity on behalf of the community and the anticipation and avoidance of conflict between neighbours. Planners themselves as the following chapters will show may be disappointed at the failure of planning to achieve its more ambitious aspirations. But the most vociferous and influential criticism now directed against planning is precisely against those aspects where it has been effective: against what is seen as the oppressive, arbitrary, time wasting and expensive enforcement of development control within a framework of obsolescent prescriptions for the long term uses of land. It is this criticism which sets the tone of current debate and puts onto the defensive all those who believe that planning can and should attempt more than the minimal night watchman's role, which even the most ardent advocate of the market accepts. There is no straightforward calculus of the costs and benefits of planning: the costs and benefits fall differently on various parties and moreover are judged by different values and priorities. The absence of agreement on the proper purposes of planning means that there can be little hope of agreement as to whether the game is worth the candle. Any practice that fails entirely to achieve what its proponents intend and imposes unacceptable costs on others would be indefensible. But planning is not in that parlous position. Once

64

the minimal case for the public control of land use has been accepted, how far it should extend and for what purposes is as much a matter of political preference as of cost effectiveness.

Notes

1 E.g. F A von Hayek's *Law, Legislation and Liberty* (London. Routledge & Kegan Paul, 1982)
   and *The Constitution of Liberty* (London. Routledge & Kegan Paul, 1960)
   John Gray *Hayek on Liberty* (Oxford. Basil Blackwell, 1984)
   Norman Barry *Hayek's Social and Economic Philosophy* (London. Macmillan, 1979)
2 E.g. R H Coase 'The Problem of Social Cost' in *The Journal of Law and Economics. Vol.III, Oct. 1960, pp 1-44*
   J M Buchanan and G Tullock *The Calculus of Consent* (Ann Arbor. University of Michigan Press, 1965)
   Mancur Olsen Jnr. *The Logic of Collective Action* (Cambridge. Harvard University Press, 1965)
3 E.g. Aaron Wildavsky 'If Planning is Everything Maybe Its Nothing' *Policy Sciences*, Vol.4, No.2 (June 1973), pp 127-153, and *The Art and Craft of Policy Analysis* (London. Macmillan, 1979)
   E Reade 'If Planning is Anything, Maybe it can be Identified' *Urban Studies* (1983) 20, pp 159-171
   Charles Lindblom *Politics and Markets* (New York. Basic Books, 1977)
   Y Dror *Public Policy Making Reexamined* (San Francisco. Chandler, 1968)
4 A Harrison *Economics and Land Use Planning* (London. Croom Helm, 1977)
5 Peter Self *Planning the Urban Region* (London. Allen & Unwin, 1983) pp 11-12
   T C Schelling in *Micromotives and Macrobehaviour* shows how neighbourhood effects can multiply the impact of individual choice to produce a pattern of residential segregation which no one actually wants.
6 Richard E Klosterman 'Arguments for and against Planning in *Town Planning Review*, Vol.56, No.1, January 1985, p 10

65

Chapter 4   What's Wrong With The System?

4.1   Criticism of the planning system is not confined to those who see anything beyond the control of nuisances and a minimum of environmental protection as misconceived and liable to be either ineffective or positively harmful. They may have the loudest, most persistent and persuasive voices at present, but among those whom we consulted there was equally firm support for a conception of planning at least as broad as that now practised. Here the major criticisms are of the failure of planning to fulfil its intentions, partly because some of the things it ought to do are beyond its powers to influence. The comments we have received are various and by no means in agreement but have concentrated on certain features of the system. In this chapter we attempt to summarise what are seen as the major shortcomings under ten heads: the inadequate scope and compass of planning, the failure to coordinate land use planning with other kinds of planning, the failure to achieve acknowledged goals of planning, the neglect of important policy considerations, differences over the distribution of the costs and benefits of planning, the absence of national policy guidance, the inappropriate structure of institutions, problems with planning powers and procedures, poor relations with the public and weaknesses in the planning profession.

The scope and compass of planning

4.2   The burden of complaint under this head is that the scope and compass of planning has been too narrow, that land use planning has had a limited role in relation to some of the major problems of our society. It is argued that planning has been too exclusively concerned with the physical environment (Bor), slow to recognise the importance of social considerations (Haar) and has failed to give adequate attention to social and economic objectives (AMA/ADC). The present compass of planning excludes important and permanent changes caused by the impact of changing agricultural practices on the landscape and upon wildlife, such as the extension of cultivation to moorland or the extension of forestry, because farmers are mistakenly assumed to be the guardians of the environment (Coppock, Wibberley, Best, Ward, Hall D, Eversley, NCC, Allison, Ramblers Association). It also excludes transport policies (AMA/ADC), highway developments and other public developments in the countryside (Coppock), and for practical purposes development by statutory undertakers and other agencies such as the water and health authorities, the Civil Aviation Authority, the Post Office, British Telecom and British Rail. There has been a failure to include within the compass of planning control some types of development, such as the pollution associated with the introduction of new technology.

4.3   On the other hand it is argued that the exercise of site specific planning control takes on too much and that attempts at social engineering are misguided. In particular planning should not concern itself with disputes between neighbours (Boynton, Burns), with the profitability of developments (BNFL), with nuclear power policy or with the character of developments which have no local environmental impact (Burns). From widely different points of the political compass, the point is made that detailed intervention through planning control rests on a misguided faith in the state as against the competence of the individual citizen (Ward, Denman, ARC).

Coordination

4.4   The major issues here are the lack of coordination between land use planning and other forms of planning, and between public sector agencies (especially those concerned with development); the fragmentation of authority and responsibility for planning; the lack of support for planning purposes from public development agencies; and the poor communication between government departments and agencies, and between tiers of government.

4.5   There is alleged to be a general lack of coordination over rural problems (Coppock), between planning, urban policy and regional planning (Burns), between physical and economic planning (Crowther, Coppock), and between housing and planning policies (Bor, Cherry). At the local authority level there is inadequate coordination between policies for planning, transport, social services, education and recreation (Bor, Cherry, Ward), and between local authorities and statutory undertakers (Burns). At the national level the Department of the Environment (DOE) and the Ministry of Agriculture Fisheries and Food (MAFF) pursue different policies for the countryside and in particular have not reached a common view of the proper balance between the claims of production and conservation (Wibberley, Thomas, CLA), and similar problems exist between the DOE and the Department of Trade and Industry over regional policy (Eversley) and the DOE and the Department of Energy (Thomas). There is a general complaint about the fragmentation of policy between government departments and their inability and lack of will to communicate (Crowther, Bor, Cherry, Eversley) which leads to ad hoc policies, loss of effectiveness and too many lines of accountability (Bancroft, Coppock, Friend, Thomas). The problems are exacerbated by the existence of too many local planning authorities (LBA, NCC), and by the separation of responsibility for forward planning from the exercise of development control (CPRE), especially in London where the local planning authorities are elected at different times. The position is made worse by a lack of awareness on the part of planners of the relationship between land use and other forms of planning (Bor, Cherry, Eversley).

4.6 There is also thought to be inadequate coordination between the public and private sectors over development (Bor) and poor cooperation with and understanding of land users by the planning profession (Denman).

Objectives I: Failure

4.7 There are two major kinds of complaint about the objectives of planning: the first is about the failure of omission and commission as regards agreed objectives and the second is about the failure to give sufficient weight to certain objectives, which is dealt with below. In general terms planning is held to have failed to contain urban sprawl and to tighten urban densities, to have failed to tackle the problems caused by traffic—congestion, noise, poor access—and to deal with atmospheric and noise pollution (Buchanan, IEHO). Planning is also said to have had little success in achieving either balanced communities (matching homes and jobs) or integrated development (seeing that services and facilities are there when needed) (Coppock). Where development has taken place it is thought to be on an inhuman scale (Cherry, Ward) and of poor aesthetic and functional quality (Bor). The policies for the control of high buildings are judged poor (Bor) and high rise housing is seen at least partly as a planning failure (Bor, Buchanan, Higgins). Slum clearance policies are criticised for the poor quality of the new housing (Bor, Boynton, Buchanan), the soulless housing estates (Burns), the concentration on public housing (Buchanan), and the poor provision of public facilities (Hall D). Large urban renewal schemes for both commercial and housing purposes are held to have been at the expense of the poor, favouring large organisations rather than the public, involving the imposition of middle class values (Ward, Ravetz, Hall D). There has also been little improvement of physical conditions in the old urban areas because procedures have become dominant, planners lack flair, and

69

resources are wrongly allocated (Hall D). The redevelopment of city centres and the building of new shopping centres are also criticised for poor design and lack of human scale (Burns, Bor). Part of the problem is seen to arise from the exercise of too much aesthetic control (Gibberd, NCC) or control of building detail by planners without the relevant training (Gibberd, Cullingworth).

Objectives II: Neglect

4.8 The most general complaint under this head is of the irrelevance of land use planning as presently practised to the main contemporary trends which will determine the problems with which planning has to deal, to wit: the growth of giant cor- porations, the shift of manufacturing industries to the countries of the third world, the growth of the nuclear industry and of other technologies deemed capable by their opponents of destroying the environment, population growth, changes in demographic struc- ture, and the centralisation of government (Cullingworth, Ravetz, Ward). It is also argued that insufficient weight is given to the conservation of vulnerable or unrenewable resources, both natural and manmade, and that not enough care is taken to assess the environmental implications of development. Some argue that there is inadequate protection against the loss of agricultural land (for example, Eversley), though others argue that agricultural land loss is not a problem (Wibberley, Best) and in any event not due to planning (Burns). The countryside generally is thought in need of greater protection (CPRE) as are some parts of our cities (Ravetz) and the impact of major developments on natural resources ought to be given more thorough attention (Coppock). By contrast there is a strong body of opinion which thinks that too much weight is now given to *preservation*, to keeping the familiar for its own sake, and that resistance to change is too successful in the planning system because of the opportunities it provides for the representatives of minority groups to exert pressure (Boynton, Buchanan, Gibberd, NCC, LBA). Preservationist attitudes are held to inhibit economic performance (CBI), to preserve the countryside in aspic and prevent necessary changes in rural areas (CLA), to frustrate imaginative design and problem solving (Gibberd), and to preserve buildings which cannot match up to contemporary requirements (Boynton, Gibberd). Furthermore some conservation measures, such as the designation of areas or zones, are counterproductive because they attract use and prejudice the character they are supposed to protect (Best). There is also a considerable body of opinion that current planning policies fail to give enough weight to problems of the distribution of wealth and opportunity, particularly to the problems of regional inequalities and the fate of declining areas. Particular stress is laid on the lack of a serious response to the problems of inner city deprivation (Bor, Coppock, Haar, Higgins) and the problems of creating robust economies in the poorer regions (Buchanan, Crowther, Higgins) because of changes in regional policy, local government failure and the inability to channel development to needy areas (Eversley, AMA/ADC), though again others argue that planning in pursuit of regional policies has forced development away from areas which suited it best (Ravetz). The planning system is unable to generate development, which is needed but not profitable, where and when it is required (LBA, AMA/ADC, RIG).

4.9   Finally there is another strong body of opinion that current planning practice gives insufficient weight to the needs of development, and does not allow in structure and local plans for the release of enough land for commercial and housing needs. Failure to release enough land for housing produces high prices, creates scarcity and inhibits the mobility of labour (CBI), especially in rural communities (CLA). There is held to be an inadequate appreciation of the development industry among planners (Boynton, Bor) which leads to the imposition of planning conditions which in turn stifle enterprise, initiative and wealth creation (Doubleday, Gibberd, CBI, CLA, ARC). The use of planning gain and the development land tax have both restricted the supply of land for development (Boynton) and the role of landownership is misunderstood by the planners (Denman). Refusal to use the market or to release public land for development in inner city areas has produced dereliction rather than development, confused planning intentions with market inclination and led to false notions of land values and land market gluts. This reflects a poor understanding of market processes in inner cities and the possible role of the market in alleviating them and of planning in exacerbating them (Denman). Finally planning has failed to grapple with the problems of land and property speculation (Crowther) and thus with the problems of costs and benefits considered next.

Costs and benefits

4.10   Here there are two separate issues: the distribution of costs and benefits of planning policies as between the public authority and the private developer and the distribution of costs and benefits as between private citizens. On the first question there is no preponderant opinion and some confusion. It is widely held that the problems of betterment and compensation have not been adequately resolved and that an agreed policy with regard to both planning gain and the taxation of development gains is necessary (Burns, Crowther, Haar, Ward, Ravetz, Hall D, Coppock, Eversley, LBA). Most are in favour of some form of development land tax and of planning gain, though one or two voices oppose betterment policies altogether (Denman) and the use of planning gain (Boynton). It is also argued that not enough attention has been given to the question of who pays the bill for the provision of urban infrastructure (for example, water supply on new residential developments) (Grant). There is considerable doubt about both the wisdom and cost of schemes like that under the Wildlife and Countryside Act which provide incentives for not undertaking development, but some support the use of incentives rather than controls as a means of ensuring desirable development (Wibberley). On the distribution of costs and benefits as between citizens, there is a widely supported view that planning policies have favoured the well off by protecting their amenity at the expense of others. Conservation policies and green belts for instance force up house prices (Crowther, Doubleday, Mandelker, Gibberd) especially for local inhabitants in rural areas (Coppock). There is an equally firm view that the costs of redevelopment have fallen heavily on the poor, as have the failures in the design of public housing (Ravetz, Hall D, Ward, Bor, Buchanan, Higgins, Burns).

National policy

4.11   There is widespread criticism of the lack of national policy guidance for planning authorities (Mandelker, Buchanan, AMA/ ADC, CPRE), the absence of a national land use plan (Burns), and frequently changing and inconsistent guidance from central government (Higgins, Buchanan). National policies are particularly inadequate in respect of energy and transport issues (NHTPC), rural depopulation, the balance between conservation and development, problems crossing local authority boundaries, such as tourism (Coppock), and for national development projects such as airports and energy installations (AMA/ADC). There is not enough policy guidance for public inquiries into major developments and public inquiries themselves are an inappropriate instrument for establishing national policies (BNFL). At the same time national government is seen to intervene too often and too directly in what are essentially local matters (Hall D, NHTPC, McConnell), but fails to provide at regional level the strategic planning functions which are beyond the competence of local planning authorities (Burns, Best, Cherry, Coppock, AMA/ADC). National government does not use regional plans for the allocation of resources or as a basis for making decisions on appeals or the approval of structure plans (Hall D). Nor does national government use regional planning to implement national policies on such matters as the distribution of population, boundary problems and the local input of national developments such as airports or power stations (CPRE).

Institutional structure

4.12   Besides the criticism of the lack of a regional structure for planning implied above, there are specific criticisms of the inappropriateness of present local government boundaries for planning purposes (Bor, McConnell, Hall P) and of the division of responsibility for plan making and development control between different tiers of local government (Burns, Hall P, RTPI). There are also frequent criticisms of the conflict, muddle and uncertainty caused by the proliferation of agencies with concurrent or overlapping functions (Bor, Hall P, Haar, Ward, Coppock, Boynton, AMA/ADC) and a general view that the distribution of powers, resources and responsibilities is incoherent (McConnell). There is also concern about the creation of non-elected special function agencies such as the Docklands Development Corporation. Although few who commented on the division of powers and functions were happy with the present local government structure in England and Wales, there seemed to be a general disposition to accept that major reorganisation of local government was out of the question in the immediate future and not as much attention was paid to the issue as we expected. This may also of course reflect the belief that institutional structures are relatively unimportant to effective planning.

Powers and procedures

4.13   A major fault of the system is the long drawn out and costly procedures both for the formulation of plans and their implementation. Structure plans take far too long to prepare (Buchanan, Crowther, Haar, NHTPC, Cherry, McConnell, Coppock) which leads to the use of informal plans and thus undermines the credibility of the system (AMA/ADC). Plans are already obsolete by the time they are produced (Ward). The procedures for development control are also cumbersome, expensive and frustrating (Buchanan, CBI, Coppock, Denning) and are much too geared to professionals, with a resultant loss of public confidence (Denning). Public participation is in itself a source of delay (Wilmott) and planning inquiries are prolonged and expensive (Bancroft, Cherry, Gibberd) especially for objectors

73

(Buchanan) and are partly prolonged by the appearance of objectors who have no direct interest (LBA).

4.14 Despite the length of time taken to produce plans, uncertainties about planning policies remain and especially about the likelihood of permission for particular developments in particular areas. Plans themselves are too vague (Boynton, Buchanan, Crowther, Allison) and too much discretion is allowed in the exercise of planning control (Cullingworth). The relaxation of previously tight controls leads to greater uncertainty and more frequent challenges to planning decision (CPRE, AMA/ADC). Some uncertainties are created because of uncertainty about government funding for infrastructure (LBA) and some because of the abuse by local planning authorities of inquiries, which they use to abrogate responsibility for decisions to avoid making policy (Gibberd).

4.15 Plans are in any event made on the wrong model, attempting to provide a blueprint for the future rather than guidelines for the handling of change (Bor, Ward, Hall P). The result is a delayed response to new problems and priorities on social issues (Bor, Haar), to the influx of immigrants (Higgins), to changes in agricultural practices (CPRE, Wibberley), to the impact of multi-national companies (Doubleday, Higgins), to multi-racial society (Haar), to the dispersal of population (Hall D), to employment trends (NCC), to economic decline (Eversley), to regional disparities, and to energy conservation (CPRE). This slowness of response is partly the result of planners' uncertainties about their professional role, of poor training and of concentration on the bread and butter work of development control (CPRE). Planning is therefore reactive, responding to problems or crises, rather than trying to anticipate them (Eversley) and shows little foresight, for instance, on emerging rural problems such as the conflicting demands of holiday makers, commuters, the retired, agricultural production and rural depopulation on the economic base of rural areas (Coppock).

4.16 There is in addition too much concern for the current problems and the immediate future at the expense of long term thinking (Burns, LBA, LGBC) and therefore not enough forward planning on such matters as minerals, green belt, and road plans (AMA/ADC). Too many decisions are made on the basis of short term (especially market) considerations (AMA/ADC, CPRE) or equally short term political expediency (Boynton, Burns, Doubleday, LBA, Coppock, McConnell).

4.17 Despite the effort that goes into producing plans, not enough concern is shown for the problems and possibilities of implementation, especially where the demand for development is weak (Bor, Crowther). The consequence is a lack of realism in forward planning (Cherry, Ward). Given the means available for the control of land use and what they can reasonably be expected to achieve, the scope of plans is much too ambitious (Boynton), especially where attempting to affect the regional distribution of employment (Mandelker, Cherry, Cullingworth) or to achieve economic growth (Burns, Ward). Plans are also too ambitious given the uncertainty of the future: much effort is wasted on development plans given the difficulty of anticipating a sufficient range of future contingencies and the many different lines of accountability for those whose actions are necessary to implement them (Friend). Implementation is weakened by inadequate powers for job creation, conservation, land purchase and design control (Bor, Hall D), and by lack of resources (Boynton, Hall D, Buchanan). The system of development control is weak (Buchanan), there are too many exceptions from development control (Mandelker) and insufficient powers to ensure that development control is exercised in compliance with structure plans (CPRE). The plans are themselves too vague to be implemented (McConnell, Eversley) and there is in addition a lack of will to implement them (Boynton, Burns). There are too many squabbles over the implementation of plans between different tiers of authority (Bancroft) and too little room for imagination and flair in the work of implementation (Bancroft, Bor, Hall D, Eversley, CPRE).

4.18 There is too much reliance on development control to implement planning proposals, especially in areas where development demand is weak: development control cannot *create* growth, only redistribute it (Cherry, LBA, Coppock), and there should be more use of incentives, carrots rather than sticks, to achieve the objectives of plans especially in rural areas (Wibberley, Coppock, CLA). There is in any event poor enforcement of planning decisions, for instance on conditions and refusals and of all environmental regulations (Allison), partly because of lack of staff, the attitudes of magistrates and problems in establishing ownership (LBA). But some planning ideas are too zealously applied, in particular the enforcement of non-conforming uses which weakens the industrial base and is particularly harmful to small businesses (Bor, Crowther, Higgins, Ward). One reason for the weaknesses in the foundation and implementation of plans is the complexity of planning legislation, which is frequently changed: new functions are tagged on without proper revision, new uses are found for old legislation, legislation is overwritten in a vain attempt to cover every detail, the attitudes of judges change, and greater use is made of subordinate legislation (Grant). The effect of the rapidity of change in planning legislation is to create self doubt and uncertainty among planners, especially about career prospects, which lead both to poor professional standards (Bancroft) and major gaps in plans (Buchanan, Burns).

4.19 In addition the information base for planning is unsatisfactory. There is not enough information on existing trends in the pattern of land use or the rate of land conversion (Best), and income and expenditure statistics for local authority areas are lacking and censuses are not frequent enough (Hall D). The research base for planning is inadequate (Eversley), the forecasting techniques are poor (Coppock) and give a spurious impression of precision (Eversley).

Public participation

4.20 The public image of planning is said to be poor (Higgins, Mandelker) because of the inability of planners to deliver on unrealistic promises (Hall D, AMA/ADC), excessive delay in producing and implementing plans, excessive jargon, and public confusion of the reponsibilities of planners with those of other local government services (NHTPC). Plans are thought to be too vague and to cover too large an area to have much meaning for the public (Crowther) and to fail to take account of the public's wishes (Doubleday, Haar, Hall D, MacRory) partly because there is little communication between planners and the public (Hall D).

4.21 Development control procedures are said to be too much geared to the professional and the articulate and to be losing public confidence (Denning), though there is considerable doubt as to whether they have ever enjoyed the confidence of the poor, who have always been the objects (and victims) of planning decisions rather than participants in them (Cherry, Ward, Coppock, LBA).

4.22 It is widely felt that planning inquiries favour the rich, the articulate and the professional but not the general public (Higgins, Buchanan, Denning, Cherry, Eversley, BNFL, Coppock), that their style of procedure is intimidating to the public (MacRory), that they take too long and are too expensive (Bancroft, Cherry, Gibberd), especially for objectors (Buchanan), and that they are abused by both national and local government as a substitute for clear policy decisions (BNFL, Gibberd). Some of these complaints are directed particularly at the exceptional large public inquiries into major national developments (Barker) but some are also directed against local inquiries. It is argued that appeal through written representations helps to exclude the public, as does the fact that neighbours have no legal right to notification of planning applications or of approvals and that local authorities cannot hold their own planning inquiries (MacRory). Public participation is also discouraged by the absence of a 'parish' tier in the system (Cherry). On the other hand there are signs that participatory democracy, particularly in the form of articulate minority pressure groups, is displacing representative democracy through elected bodies in the planning process (NCC, Wilmott).

The planning profession

4.23   There are complaints about the poor quality of the planners themselves (Bor, CPRE, Coppock, Doubleday, Cullingworth), and the quality of the education they receive (Bancroft), about poor links between research and practice (Bor), about the lack of training in planning for politicians (Hall D, Gibberd), about the lack of well-qualified design professionals (Gibberd), the failure to use consultants (Gibberd, Bor), and about the urban bias of training which leaves the profession ill adapted to cope with the problems of rural planning (Coppock).

4.24   There are also complaints of poor management in planning departments: of poor communication, insufficient delegation and lack of motivation for staff (McConnell).

Conclusion

4.25   This bare recital has not revealed the arguments behind the complaints, but it has perhaps suggested one important thing; that most of those we have consulted, however critical of the present system, both place a heavy responsibility on planning and entertain high expectations of what it may achieve. In the next chapter we provide a rather more detailed guide to the positive suggestions for change to redress the perceived shortcomings of the system and to realise the potential which most of the critics believe to be there. In the following section we shall analyse the assumptions and attitudes underlying the suggestions and attempt an anatomy of the political positions they reveal.

Chapter 5 What Should Be Done About It?

5.1   The cures prescribed reflect the ailments diagnosed, but a similar diagnosis does not necessarily result in a common prescription: the answer to a particular failing of the system may be more of the same or less. In this necessarily brief summary of the many proposals that have been put to us, we shall concentrate on the specific: if a complaint of lack of coordination between different kinds of planning is followed by a demand for more coordination, we need to know how exactly it is to be brought about. Differences about the future of planning can arise as readily from different estimates of the feasibility of particular procedures or institutional arrangements as from differences of interest, though we suspect that differences of the first kind are closely related to differences of the second.

The scope and compass of planning

5.2   There are general proposals for greater clarification of the various responsibilities for planning (ADC/AMA) and for the separation of these responsibilities into separate though closely related kinds of planning: environmental planning (the maintenance of standards and quality), public plans and programmes (development, investment, inner city programmes and so forth), special initiatives (enterprise zones, new towns), regional planning (coordination at regional level) (Cherry). But the major proposals for change in the scope of the planning system concern the rural areas; and the first and most important of these is the proposal to extend development control to agricultural developments such as buildings for intensive livestock rearing, changes in the use of wetland or moorland, hedge removal, new drainage schemes and tree planting and felling (Wibberley, CPRE, Higgins, Allison, Ramblers Association, Burns, Buchanan, GBC). Although there is wide support for this proposal, it should be emphasised that this is not support for a blanket extension of development control to all changes in the use of agricultural land. As Wibberley puts it: 'It is superficially easy to ask for an extension of statutory land use controls across the broad and varied landscape of rural land use. It is, however, also very easy to see how ineffective and foolish this could become if it interferes with season to season and day to day alterations in land use required by normal farm husbandry. . . . The

79

only kind of statutory land use controls that will work in the British farming scene today will be those loosely affecting permanent structures like farm buildings, long term land use changes such as tree planting and felling, major drainage schemes and, possibly, the ploughing up or drastic surface treatment of rough grazings or long established permanent pastures. Even those will need knowledgeable and sympathetic handling by local planning offices, backed up by technical and economic agricultural expertise'. A related proposal is that farmers intending to make significant landscape changes should be obliged to notify the local planning authority and that the authority should have the power to impose a 'stop notice' (RTPI, CPRE). There are several proposals relating to rural planning which are more properly dealt with under other heads, but two follow directly from the proposal to extend development control to agricultural land use, whose main aim is to increase the weight given to the interests of conservation. Both proposals are made by Professor Wibberley and their intention is to persuade the farmer of the case for conservation and to enlist his support and experience in its cause. The first is to establish committees, drawn from the farming community and relevant public bodies, to give advice on conservation, to make grants and to decide on priorities and on the appropriate balance between incentives, penalties and controls. The second is for the Ministry of Agriculture Fisheries and Food (MAFF) to establish an advisory service for farmers on matters of rural conservation. There are some who would put more emphasis on control than on persuasion, and a few who would resist the extension of controls altogether, and they probably speak for a large majority of landowners and farmers though views are changing rapidly.

Coordination

5.3   There is predictably much support for greater coordination of town and country planning with social and economic planning both within and between public authorities (Bor, Burns, Higgins, CPRE, Hall D, ADC). At local authority level this means the adoption of a corporate approach to planning (McConnell), which would involve a programme for allocating land, manpower and capital resources and establishing priorities for the allocation of land and the provision of infrastructure (RTPI). Greater coordination must be achieved by requiring the local planning authority, the private sector and the community to produce a 'community plan' (Cullingworth), local planning authorities should be given greater control over public sector developments like highways (Bor), and structure plans should provide the basis for coordinating all public agency policies at the county level (CPOS). It is also argued that it would help to have a clear demarcation of planning functions between different tiers of government (MPOS), that all planning matters should be carried out at a single level of local governemnt (Burns), and that strategic planning functions should be transferred from water and health authorities to the upper tier of local government (MPOS). All these proposals are designed to overcome the problems deriving from the division of responsibility for closely related policies between different tiers and kinds of authority. The same thought lies behind Lord Bancroft's suggestion that 'it was a profound mistake to split off the transport activities of DOE into a separate Department'. It is however impossible and self-defeating to attempt to bring all functions and policies under one roof. Hence it is argued that the impact of other government policies on rural planning should be anticipated by requiring prior approval by counties (or the Scottish or Welsh offices) of all government grants and loans for developments in rural areas (Thorburn, RTPI, CPOS), and that the MAFF should accept fiscal responsibility for the environmental consequences of its incentive schemes (CPOS). Whatever structure or division of functions is adopted, there will always be boundary problems, both physical and functional, which will require both a hierarchy of authority and a means of adjudication. Hence the importance of the suggestions of Andrew Thorburn. First: 'Local planning authorities should be obliged to accommodate in their structure or local plans any policies or proposals which have been published by the government and relevant public bodies, unless it is impracticable to do so'. And second: 'Local planning authorities should be required to call for an Inspector or person appointed through the Inspectorate to act as an informed arbitrator in cases of unresolved differences with another public body, and be encouraged to do so where the difference is with a private interest'.

Objectives

5.4 We have identified in the evidence four major objectives which it is thought should be given more weight in planning: conservation, the quality of the built environment, economic and social development. These are not necessarily compatible with each other and there is indeed a significant divergence of opinion about the proper role of planning in relation to development. This divergence appears to reflect both a difference of political view and a difference of experience between those planners who are still dealing with pressures for development from the market (mainly in the South East) and those working in areas where 'spontaneous' development has practically ceased.

81

5.5   Before exploring that difference further we should note that the complaint about the lack of concern for conservation is reflected in proposals that more effort and resources should be devoted to it (Allison, Thorburn), and that there should be no weakening of powers of control needed for conservation purposes, for the prevention of bad design and the waste of resources (RTPI). To ensure that adequate attention is paid to such factors, Dr Ravetz has suggested that all new development proposals should be assessed according to four balance sheets—to reflect the implications of the development in terms of the ecology, economic activity, social benefit and finance—and that budgets should be drawn up setting out the risks, costs and waste involved in any development. Others suggest that environmental impact assessments (EIAs) should be carried out for all substantial projects either before a public inquiry (Hall D) or on application (NCC). In rural areas it is however argued that conservation should not inhibit all development and that more emphasis should be placed on the stimulation of economic activity (CLA, Coppock), that there should be less constraint on housing developments in villages where there is clearly a demand related to their businesses and employment opportunities (CLA) and that in general more sensitive initiatives to provide housing and employment for residents should be undertaken (CPRE).

5.6   There is a strongly held but controverted view that the main purpose of planning should be to maintain and enhance the quality of the built environment. Powers both of regulation and promotion should be used to ensure an efficient and agreeable environment, but should not be used as a means to achieve other goals such as the redistribution of wealth. Planning should concentrate on the design and appearance of buildings and their surrounding spaces and leave economic and social policy to be implemented by other more appropriate institutions (Burns). To improve the quality of urban design, more should be done to bridge the gap between architects and planners (Bor, Gibberd), local planning authorities should make more use of architects and design consultants, and competitions should be encouraged for buildings of exceptional importance (Gibberd) and conducted accorded according to RIBA guidelines (RIBA). Amenity requires both protection, such as the long term guarantee of the sanctity of green belts (LGBC) and enhancement through increased efforts to reclaim derelict land (Higgins), and requirements for environmental schemes in general improvement areas and housing action areas. More use should be made of EIAs (Bor, RTPI), and of development briefs for key sites (CPOSW) and statutory undertakers should be obliged to consult local planning authorities on developments like road works and their environmental consequences (Gibberd). Finally there are suggestions for local environmental wardens (Gibberd), for a 'National Environment Service' to enforce environmental regulations, to promote and carry out environmental improvements, and to provide employment (Allison), for a standing Royal Commission on the Environment, on the lines of the Royal Commission on Environmental Pollution, to maintain the effectiveness of environmental policies (Thomas).

5.7 A quite different emphasis is called for by those who see planning as both too reactive and too restrictive. Several important bodies such as the London Boroughs Association (LBA), the Royal Town Planning Institute (RTPI), the Association of District Councils (ADC) and the Association of Metropolitan Authorities (AMA) argue that there is a need for a more positive and promotional role for planning, which involves identifying and promoting investment opportunities and requires strengthened powers, more resources and a more secure framework for public sector investment. Local planning authorities should be given increased powers and funds to implement plans (ADC/AMA), to purchase land (Hall D), to restore and revitalise the nation's ageing infrastructure (CPRE), and to regenerate the inner city (Burns). To do this requires a change of attitude towards development, which sees the role of planning authorities as enabling rather than controlling, coupled with a better understanding of the role of private developers and of local community institutions (Burns), with more modest and less severe controls (Denning, ARC). Local planning authorities should take the initiative by greater use of development briefs, by giving greater encouragement to development in enterprise zones beyond relaxing controls (Haar), by the production of area development programme plans which provide for the release of public sector land, the provision of infrastructure and land development (CPOSW). When there are more or less permanent policies of restraint, for instance within a national park, a reversal of the normal presumption in favour of development might be considered to prevent unacceptable development, 'whilst enabling acceptable development to proceed with the minimum of extra cost and bureaucratic intervention' (ADC/AMA).

5.8 For some this implies a more positive view of the role of private enterprise, of local planning authorities cooperating and assisting rather than controlling the private sector (Denman, CBI, ARC, Moor). This requires in the first place that more account be taken of the economic consequences of decisions on development control (CBI) and that there should be more pre-application advice to developers from local planning authorities (Crowther). There should also be a greater willingness on the part of local planning authorities to enter into partnership arrangements with the private sector for redevelopment projects (RTPI) to dispose of publicly owned land and to subsidise private developers willing to risk capital in the inner city (Denman).

5.9 These suggestions reflect the view that current planning procedures place a severe burden on developers, inhibit adaptation and change, stifle enterprise and threaten the prospects of economic growth or wealth creation. It is readily apparent that there are differences about what should be included within the definition of wealth. But there is a further and more fundamental difference about the purpose of planning. As David Eversley puts it: 'We have to come to a view as to whether planning is a means of redistributing real incomes, life chances, and environmental quality, or whether it is merely a means of preventing gross injury to particular individuals or communities'. When we talk of positive planning we have to distinguish between planning that takes a positive view of the market, while attempting to correct inefficiences, and planning that takes a positive role in attempting to redress the inequalities of the market and to make good its omissions by measures to increase the access of the disadvantaged to housing, health, recreation and communal activity. This is one of the most important of the dimensions of disagreement which we shall analyse in the following part of this Report.

Costs and benefits

5.10 Compensation and betterment are generally recognised to be difficult subjects. There is support for a more determined attempt to collect betterment (Haar, Eversley, Bor). As far as planning gain is concerned the LBA points out that it is a matter of doubt as to whether bargaining for gain by a local authority is intra vires since a S.52 agreement cannot be made a condition of a grant planning permission (DOE Circular 5/68, paragraph 34). The LBA goes on to suggest that there is an argument for a statutory obligation to consider planning gain for certain classes of development, such as major non-domestic sites, not just in relation to the site itself, but by contributions to the development of other land. The case for planning gain is by no means universally accepted and some see it not only as a discouragement to developers but as a misapprehension of the ways in which public benefits derive from private investment (CBI, ARC, Buchanan). There is support for the idea that a proportion of development land tax should be channelled to local authorities, partly in order to strengthen their

84

fiscal base (Hall D), partly to provide resources for compensation required under other areas of planning law (LBA), and partly to reduce the temptation to planners to press for planning gain (Boynton). We sense that there would have been widespread support for the plea of the LBA to preserve 'the present Development Land Tax Act which at least has the merit of stability as the machinery is well understood having at least survived the election of a new Parliament completely opposed to the views of its predecessor'. But alas the plea was in vain and the question is once again open.

5.11 Two proposals have been made to us regarding compensation: first that there should be a review of the compensation code so that the price paid for land purchased by a public authority approximates to its existing use value (Hall D); and second that compensation for curtailing 'existing use rights' (Schedule 8 and Article 4 Directions) should no longer be paid (LBA).

National policy

5.12 There are two distinct but connected lines of argument in our evidence about national policy and the role of central government in planning. The first is that central governemnt should provide much clearer guidance on its policy over a wide range of issues which impinge on planning. The second is that central government should interfere less both in plan making and in the exercise of development control. More national policy guidance is called for on the distribution of population and employment, defence installations, natural resources and the countryside, rural land use and the preservation of agricultural land, mineral resource exploitation, major developments in such fields as transport, energy, minerals, key locations' for such developments, and on acceptable types of development generally (variously Haar, DPOS, CPRE, CPOSW, Coppock, Thorburn, MPOS, Allison, NCC, RTPI, and BNFL).

5.13 More ambitious ideas are mooted by the RTPI which argues: 'An integrated planning system would require a willingness on the part of central government to plan at national and regional level, for national aspirations to be articulated and resource allocations to be prepared on a realistic basis of 3 to 5 year programmes'. There is some scepticism about the possibility of a national land use strategy, if that implies something more than the existence of a set of country structure plans covering the whole country and approved by the DOE (Best). But Professor Coppock finds it 'extraordinary that planning nationally should be achieved very largely by a "bottom up" approach, i.e. simply by piecing together all the local authority plans, with little more than attempts to see that they match at the edges. I believe that there should be a National Structure Plan in which central government expresses its priorities and defines what is important nationally. Developments in Scotland have made some progress in this direction in the issue of national policy guidelines, but those deal with each issue separately and the overall political perspective of such a plan is lacking'.

5.14   Even without achieving as much as this, it should be possible where particular national policies are clearly articulated to see that they are incorporated or accommodated in structure and local plans (Thorburn), and the Metropolitan Planning Officers Society (MPOS) argues : 'Central government should accept the responsibility of drawing together its policies that impinge on land use, and publish regular guidelines at national and regional level. Its power to vary local planning authority decisions on either development plans or planning applications should be restricted by statute to that necessary to achieve conformity with such published guidance'. This view is supported by the County Planning Officers Society (CPOS) in their observation on structure planning: 'Government should intervene only where there is a departure from approved policy which impinges on the national interest or where arbitration is needed'. Andrew Thorburn in his 'Proposals for a better planning system' goes further and argues that alterations to a structure plan 'should be approved by the authority responsible for their preparation and not the Secretary of State. The panel conducting an examination in public into a structure plan alteration should be appointed and briefed by the Secretary of State, but should report to the structure plan authority which would be obliged to take its views into account in approving the plan'.

5.15   The same line of argument is linked by Professor Donnison to the case for greater local autonomy thus: 'There may be a case for giving greater powers to planners and local planning authorities . . . subject to less pervasive rights of appeal, but that case will only be a strong one if clear policy guidelines derived from recognised procedures for public debate are first promulgated by the central and (in Scotland) the regional authorities. The Scottish Regional Reports, effectively abolished by the present Government, could, if required, provide an important part of the framework for that debate and the guidelines to be derived from it. Objectors to planning decisions falling within the fields covered by such guidelines would then be entitled to appeal only if they could show that relevant guidelines had not been taken into account when decision were made about proposals for redevelopment'.

5.16 The positive case for more local authority initiative within a clearly articulated framework of national policy arises both from the greater urgency, sensitivity and understanding of the local economic crises produced by public expenditure cuts and sluggish activity in the private sector, which have undermined the traditional basis of planning, and also from the fact that central government initiatives like enterprise zones are necessarily exceptional (Cullingworth). Whether local government with its present structure, financing and treatment by central government can respond, is another matter.

Institutional structure

5.17 For planning, the region is the missing link in the institutional structure. There are of course plenty of bodies operating at a regional level, but they are either outposts of central government or functional agencies only loosely connected to the planning system. And yet many of the problems with which planning has to grapple can only be resolved at a level somewhere between the local authority and the country as a whole. Hence the perennial attraction of a regional tier of government, which is fully reflected in our evidence, despite the indifference or hostility of Whitehall and Town Hall not to speak of County Hall. The strong version of regionalism refers back to the Memorandum of Dissent to the Report of the Royal Commission on the Constitution which proposed elected regional authorities taking on some of the regional functions of central government, responsibility for water and health, and the planning functions of county councils. They would be responsible for producing comprehensive social, economic, and physical plans. As a probable corollary, the upper tier of existing local government would disappear and a unitary system of most purpose local authorities, with rather wider boundaries than the present districts, would absorb those county functions not transferred to the region. The regional authorities would have the responsibility and it is hoped the clout to bring into the planning framework not only the health and water authorities but the public utilities and other statutory undertakers and corporations such as the Civil Aviation Authority, the Post Office, British Telecom and British Rail (Crowther, Doubleday, CPRE, Hall D, Bor, Eversley).

5.18 Weaker variations on the same theme suggest regional planning councils indirectly elected or nominated by local authorities and central government (Higgins) or bodies in each region on the model of the Standing Conference for London and South East Regional Planning, with permanent staffs, elected members from the local authorities and a plan-making function: 'Environmental priorities should be put squarely within their terms of reference. Regional objectives for future land uses and social and economic development could then be offered for public discussion and agreed. These would then be enacted through county structure plans and district local plans with the regional body exercising oversight over the implementation of the strategy' (CPRE). Minimalist regional proposals requiring no legislation or institutional reform have been put forward by Andrew Thorburn as a means of 'ensuring that the separate investment programmes and priorities of nationalised industries, government departments, statutory bodies and local authorities are in step and not in wasteful conflict with one another. They also seek to identify the effects of government policies upon the economy or environment of each part of the country'. The first proposal is that the departments, major agencies', and authorities which use public resources for investment should meet twice a year in each region, under the chairmanship of a junior minister, to examine development programmes, priorities and policies affecting planning in the region and ensure that adequate advice about their consequences is available. And the second that central and local governments, acting together, should prepare an analysis of facts and trends relating to planning in each region and present this to Parliament annually, for discussion in a select committee. The second proposal is close to the Scottish regional report system, which is no longer mandatory, but which the RTPI considers should either be made mandatory again or replaced by extending the scope of the present limited structure plans. A further proposal deriving from Scottish and Welsh experience is for regional development agencies for the English regions (Crowther).

5.19   Apart from the regional dimension, there is considerable unhappiness about the present structure of local government, the division of planning functions between counties and districts, the relation of plan making to development control, and the failure to coordinate policy for local authority services with structure planning. A specific proposal from the Council for the Protection of Rural England (CPRE) is that county planning authorities should have returned to them adequate powers to ensure that policies in approved structure plans are implemented by district councils in a way that secures strategic planning objectives. County powers to certify that local plans accord with approved structure plan policies remain one important check in the system. But CPRE supports a return to the county councils of the powers of direction over certain categories of planning application handled by districts, which they enjoyed before the Local Government, Planning and Land Act 1980. Even those who are pessimistic about the prospect of any major reorganisation of sub-national government think that some enlargement in present district boundaries would be an improvement (Bor) and especially those of the largest former county boroughs outside the metropolitan cities, such as Plymouth, Leicester and Southampton (RTPI).

5.20 And finally behind all considerations of changing boundaries and functions lurks the spectre of local government finance. No one has had the temerity to venture a proposal and perhaps the last word can be left with David Eversley: 'The attempt was made in the 1970s to reform the rating system; no sensible proposals emerged and the report commissioned by the government of the day sank without trace. Despite this past failure, the reorganisation of local government finance will have to be tackled, not only on the grounds of fairness and justice, but also because without such a reformed system, planning cannot function'.

Powers and procedures

5.21 Proposals about planning procedures relate closely to opinions about the scope and purposes of planning, but there seems to be a general impatience with the slowness of the system. Various suggestions have been made to limit the need to get planning permission at all. One is for a relaxation of the general development order (GDO) to widen the category of permitted development (Boynton, Burns) and this is linked to suggestions for greater use of the law of nuisance, 'of the courts, of codes for the protection of neighbours especially for 'developments' not requiring planning permission, and the adoption of precisely specified planning standards as legal requirements, on such matters as daylighting, privacy and access (Boynton, Cullingworth, CLA). Others argue that local authorities should be enabled to employ special development orders to extend the range of permitted development which would not require planning permission (ADC/AMA), and some would go further to advocate a zoning system on the American model, where there is no need for planning permission unless a development is contrary to the plan (LDEC). Proposals of this kind, for simplified planning zones or enterprise zones, seem most often to arise from sympathy with the problems which delay and uncertainty present to the large developer. From the other end of the scale there is a 'modest recommendation' from Colin Ward for a 'planning holiday': 'That certain areas should be experimentally designated as plan-free zones and exempted from development control . . . it is also necessary that they should be similarly exempted from the operation of building regulations'. Mr Ward, encouraged by the example of 'cities the poor build' in the Southern Hemisphere, is concerned to release the enterprise, initiative and imagination of ordinary people in the creation of their own environment, and believes that DIY new towns with site and service arrangements but no planning controls would enable this to happen.

5.22 The limitation of planning controls to essentials has wider support, which includes suggestions to exclude questions of design where an architect has been involved (Gibberd, RIBA), and to exclude the profitability of a scheme as a consideration (BNFL). Other suggestions for avoiding delay include a reduction in the amount of detail required in outline planning applications (RIBA), a single procedure for building regulations and development control (Cullingworth) and a requirement on planning applicants to show that they have made the required statutory consultations before making an application (Pwllheli). And Sir John Boynton feels so strongly about delay that he would like to impose some sanctions on the planners: 'My final criticism is that the present system tilts the scales too much against the developer. The planners can and do delay consideration of applications. They may be holding out for planning gain. They are usually convinced that they know best. The developer who does not like their ideas has the heavy costs and considerable delay and uncertainty of an appeal. If you win there is no way of recouping your losses—the legal and expert witness costs, the interest charges, the lost market or opportunity. With the highest of motives and a firm belief in their own infallibility, planners can be quite unscrupulous in black-mailing developers into submission. The architect or developer who can sing with Sinatra "I did it my way" is a rara avis. Something needs to be done to redress the balance, perhaps including:

(a) automatic costs for winning an appeal;
(b) compensation for proved loss flowing from failure to decide within the statutory period—perhaps coupled with a notice to the planning authority to start the compensation time clock running.'

5.23 Closely related to the question of delay is the question of certainty and here there are important differences of view. Some argue that structure and local plans should be less broad, general and vague (LBA), that there is a need for more certainty in policies of planning restraint (CPRE), and that the degree of discretion in the exercise of development control should be reduced, possible by the abolition of the 'other material considerations' component, so that development decisions have to be made on the basis of statutory plans (MPOS, Cullingworth). Against the demand for certainty there is an equally strong plea for greater flexibility in planning; the difficulty of forecasting and the unavoidable uncertainties about the future require that planning should proceed a step at a time, that each step should close down as few alternatives as possible, and that each step should be capable of being stopped and changed at any time (Friend, Bor, RTPI, Eversley, Burns, ADC). As the MPOS puts it: 'The planning profession should ditch the single "blueprint" notion of plans in favour of an approach which can cope better with uncertainty. The "continuous planning" model is capable of providing a suitable balance between flexibility and firm guidance. It requires no specific changes in legislation, only in attitudes and administrative practice. Moreover it is the direction in which plans that are taken seriously are already evolving—for example the corporate plans of major industrial concerns'. A specific recommendation to this end is for the formal review of structure and local plans every two years (Thorburn). It is recognised that this style of plan making depends on a change in present interminable procedures for approving plans. There is a related argument for planning to pay more attention to questions of implementation, with greater emphasis on what is achievable, on the availability of resources in the short term (Bor, ADC/AMA, Hall D) and more attention to the costs of implementation at the plan making stage (MPOS).

5.24 Two further kinds of suggestion are made to enhance the effectiveness of planning decisions, which is said to require more staff and resources and possibly the imposition of strict liability and fixed penalties for specific contraventions of enforcement or stop notices, and a statutory requirement for full information from landowners in enforcement cases (LBA). The second involves the more general question of the information base for plan making, which evokes demands for the use of better forecasting and evaluation techniques (MPOS, Boynton, CPOS), a national survey of land use stocks and flows (Best, Coppock), a ten yearly land use census and a five yearly population census, a regular census of employment (CPOS), and an annual micro-census of the kind used in Northern Ireland (RTPI). The Ordnance Survey whose 'large scale maps are the foundation on which the whole edifice of town and country planning is built' should be protected from commercialisation (Bancroft) and the Land Registry and land ownership records should be opened to the public (LBA). There should also be more information on newer forms of development (CPOS) and more effort to encourage and develop work on disaggregating national economic forecasts to regional and sub-regional levels (Simmie).

Public participation

5.25 Perhaps because of the concern about the incipient conflict between elected local authorities and pressure groups, there is some support for a local or community tier of government for planning purposes and certainly a desire to find ways in which people can make an active contribution towards the planning of their own immediate environment (Wilmott, Bor, Ravetz, Hall D). It is felt that there should be more experiment with participation exercises (Thomas) as a means of developing a consensus rather than simply as a means of registering protest or objection (ADC/AMA). There should therefore be more support for public funds for planning aid and advice services (Ravetz, Hall D) and a duty on those who initiate plans to ensure that those who are directly affected by the plans are separately represented at planning inquiries (Ravetz). Information is an essential precondition of participation and there should be a general obligation on local planning authorities to publicise all local planning documents and invite representations and to hold a public inquiry, hearing or arbitration if this is necessary in order to obtain independent advice upon a particular difference of view. Before any local planning documents are prepared a statement should be drawn up by the local planning authority responsible setting out as simply as possible the reason for their preparation, the outline brief for each, and as much of their contents as arises from structure plan policies, proposals and priorities (Thorburn). Likewise it should be a duty to give reasons for planning decisions which can be understood and judged by the public and not obscured by mystifying jargon (LBA). The planning activities of MAFF and the water authorities ought to be as open as structure planning (CPOS, RTPI) and negotiations on S.52 planning agreements ought to be more open to public scrutiny (Devon Conservation Forum). Besides making more information available, local planning authorities should make it their business to supplement exercises in participation and consultation by exploiting market research to get a better idea of what the public wants (MPOS, Boynton).

5.26 Although there is support for greater opportunity, encouragement and resources for public contribution to the process of making plans, there are some misgivings about the fact that most public participation consists in reaction against specific planning proposals even where these are in conformity with a duly approved plan. It has been suggested that the right to make objections to planning proposals might be curtailed where the objectors had previously made representations on the planning policy involved (Doubleday), or where clearly recognised procedures for public debate on the policy had been followed (Donnison); or that after participation in the formulation of policy, objections at the application stage should be limited to certain specific matters such as design and siting (ADC/AMA).

5.27 Local public inquiries perhaps raise fewer and less difficult problems than the small number of inquiries into major national development which have become a separate focus of concern. Nevertheless there are proposals to change the status of local inquiries. Lord Denning would like to replace them by a system of judicial tribunals with power to decide all issues of fact and policy: and with an appeal to the High Court on points of law only. The tribunal should consist of a panel of three—a legal chairman, a county magistrate and a chartered surveyor or planning expert. The legal chairman should be of a standing commensurate with the case and the tribunal would be seen to be independent of the ministry. Others would also like to make the planning inspectorate constitutionally independent of the minister, making decisions with regard only to his published guidance on policy maters and to the development plan (MPOS), and responsible to standing commissions whose remit would include decisions on planning appeals, called in applications, compulsory purchase orders, presentation orders, in line with the policies of central government, as well as the conduct of public inquiries into proposals by government departments, local authorities and other public bodies (Thorburn). It has also been suggested that there might be some advantage in giving inquiry powers to local authorities themselves to hold inquiries or perhaps less formal hearings into development applications (MacRory).

5.28 The central issue for the major national development is the propriety of using a local land use inquiry as the vehicle for the examination (and indeed discovery) of national policy. One solution is to exclude discussion of national issues altogether (BNFL) and another to attempt to separate them from local issues and to conduct the inquiry in two stages (Thorburn, ADC/AMA, Donnison). It is also suggested that use should be made of the Planning Inquiry Commission with a wider remit which would allow the investigation of alternative locations for a particular development or alternative means of achieving the same end (Hall

D). There are also several more detailed suggestions for improving the procedure of inquiries, in the interest both of efficiency and of legitimacy, such as that inspectors (or panels) should have power to commission research or evidence, that there should be public assistance to objectors, limits on the length of inquiries, a curtailment of rights of cross examination, less formal procedures and a smaller role for lawyers and for the use of adversarial techniques for the testing of evidence. We are of course aware that significant developments have taken place since we received evidence, both in the internal conduct of inquiries (notably at Sizewell) and in the government's subsequent handling of the report from the Stansted inquiry. The central conundrum remains and will do so until government is prepared to grasp the nettle and think about it as a constitutional issue rather than a political one.

The planning profession

5.29 There are two primary concerns about the role of the profession. The first concerns the relationship between planners and politicians and the second that between planners and the public. There are serious reservations about the development of pressure group or participatory politics in planning and a desire to reaffirm the authority of elected politicians. The greater politicisation of local government is deplored by some, but the proper relationship of planners to politicians is reaffirmed on conventional lines: it is for politicians to decide on planning objectives and for planners to display the alternatives and to advise on whether and how it is possible to achieve them (Bor, Coppock). Much more radical views of the planner's role are implicit in some of the evidence (for example, that from RIG) but these do not take the form of specific proposals and, as we shall argue below, do not appear to have a clearly articulated basis of legitimacy: that is to say that it is not clear whether the influence of the planner is to derive from the delegated authority of the politician, from professional knowledge and skills, or from some direct link with the people or special understanding of their needs. There is also some concern about the education of planners and a view that it should place more emphasis on the skills required to communicate with the public (Ravetz).

5.30 Both these concerns reflect the fact that as the scope of planning has broadened, its political salience has increased and planners find themselves pig in the middle between the public and elected representatives. As a result their position has become more exposed and more hazardous. Although this has been the primary concern of the comments made to us on the profession, it is clear that many of the criticisms of other aspects of planning have implications for the profession and are reflected in the soul searching about its education which fills the planning journals.

Conclusion

5.31   This rapid excursion can only have given a flavour of the evidence presented to us. We hope however that it is a fair representation of the range of opinion, not only in that evidence, but in the greater corpus of writing about the planning system, on which we shall also draw in the attempt to distinguish first the main lines of disagreement and secondly the planning philosophies which they reflect.

PART III   ANALYSIS

Chapter 6   The Dimensions of Disagreement

6.1   In the informal discussions which we held with a variety of people drawn from the planning profession, the development industry, central and local government and the universities, we were struck repeatedly by two things. The first was a desire to assume a consensus; to believe that right thinking people are agreed on the proper role of planning. And the second a reluctance to be explicit about the assumptions on which this supposed consensus is based, and an unwillingness to examine their implications for the principles and practices of planning. Reforms are of course often advocated without a full examination of their effects or any careful attempt to estimate their costs as well as their benefits. What we discern however is something more than failure to think through the full implications of particular suggestions: we have the impression that there is a more deep seated reluctance to tackle fundamental issues, based perhaps on the suspicion that such inquiry will reveal the extent of the disagreement which everyone wants to avoid. Before presenting our own conclusions, we think it may be useful to examine more closely and to comment on the dimensions of this disagreement, and to see in the following chapter how these differences of view combine to form a number of identifiable and incompatible positions on the proper role of planning.

6.2   At the risk of oversimplifying, these dimensions relate to the following issues:

The possibility of a 'neutral' planning system;
General attitudes to 'the market';
The most appropriate level of government for planning;
Its scope;
Its main social prescriptions;
Its style and the instruments the planning system uses to implement its plans or proposals;
The planning system's democratic base;
Its institutional form;
Its professional orientation;

The principal clients of the planning system and of the professionals operating it;
The most appropriate timescale for planning;
The geographical variation in the planning system.

Each of these issues is considered in turn. There is considerable overlap between many of them but since not all people come to the same conclusions on each it is necessary to distinguish between them. It should be noted here that while the principal purpose of this chapter is to identify the sources of disagreement, we shall comment on each in passing.

A 'neutral' town and country planning system

6.3 Is it possible to design a planning system which is politically neutral? The majority of evidence accepts that planning is highly political in the sense that it is invariably guided by views on the sort of environment which people would *like* to have. At the most fundamental level, the goals of planning, as an activity carried out largely by and for government, are ethical or moral in nature. That much at least attracts a good measure of support. The question here, however, is rather different; it is asking whether or not it is possible to design a single legal and administrative system, to form a framework for planning of sufficient flexibility so that it can be used by different political parties or groups for their different purposes. Is it possible to devise a planning system which is sufficiently adaptable to be used by both Conservative and Labour governments, for example, or does each party in power inevitably have to change the system anew each time it takes up office?

6.4 There is evidently a difference of opinion on this issue or else a reluctance to recognise its importance. Most people, when pressed, seem to think it would be advantageous if such a system could be devised and indeed that this should be our aim in reforming the planning system. It would provide a core of certainty and stability to planning which is considered to be a desirable end in itself. Others, however, believe such an ideal is fanciful and impossible to achieve in practice. Not only does each new party in power manipulate the planning system to suit its own purposes, but it also finds it has to change the system; the system itself (the legal and institutional structures upon which planning is based) has to be changed.

6.5 We are inclined to side with the sceptics. The widespread assumption that men of goodwill but of different political persuasions should be able to agree on the fundamentals of the planning system is an illusion whose staying power reflects the strength of the immediate post war political consensus on the purposes of planning. As that consensus has broken down, there has been a reluctance to recognise that the institutions created to express and implement it are no longer sustained by a common vision or political purpose. There is now an inherited body of law, procedure, convention and practice which is an institutional fact and with which we have to work. There are technical adjustments which may help those institutions to work better, and we shall suggest some. The root of the matter is however not technical but political: what planning requires is political agreement and the re-creation of a consensus on the aims it is supposed to achieve and its capacity to achieve them. It is important to recognise that the breakdown of the post war consensus results as much from disillusion with the capacity of planning as with its aims and that agreement on what we can reasonably expect of planning is fundamental to any reform of the system. But we acknowledge that the choice of means is also political and that the priority which people attach to the achievement of certain aims will determine the costs they are prepared to incur to achieve them. Thus while our own recommendations may concentrate largely on questions of institutional structure and procedure we do not regard them as technical or politically neutral.

General attitudes to the market

6.6   The second important issue over which disagreement arises concerns the degree of faith people have in the role of *markets* and especially in their efficiency and their fairness. To simplify, one group believes that free markets tend to be both efficient in allocating resources and fair in distributing goods, and thus sees the need for a minimum of public intervention. To these 'non-plan' advocates there is merit in reducing the breadth of planning, for instance, by widening the general development order's (GDO's) categories of permitted development and by enabling greater use of special development orders, and in limiting its role to that of environmental 'damage control'. Another group believes that whilst land use and real property markets are reasonably or, at least, potentially efficient, more often than not they produce unfair results. To many of these 'social market' advocates planning can itself cause unnecessary inefficiencies in the market place—by causing extra delays in the development process for example. Efforts should therefore be made to speed up the intervention process, say by simplified planning zones, or to exclude it from matters where the market knows 'best' such as the profitability of development projects or aesthetic design. The role of planning in this view would be concentrated on redistributing resources, on guiding and channelling rather than fettering market processes.

6.7 Yet another group suggests that markets tend to be inefficient but reasonably fair. Intervention is often required on the grounds of the 'public interest', because the whole community rather than any particular group is disadvantaged by particular market processes or outcomes. Indeed supporters of this line often argue that planning can often itself produce or exacerbate inequality in our society. Green belts, for example, favour the well off.

6.8 Finally, there are those who see the markets which are relevant to planning as both inefficient and unfair. This group tends to advocate at least a subservient role for market systems in relation to planned intervention, and often a more complete 'command' type economy. To this group there are distinct advantages to be had from widening the frontiers of planning control.

6.9 In our view any evaluation of the worth of markets as a means of allocating resources must be pragmatic: it really does depend on the circumstances and conditions prevailing in the market place at particular times and in particular places. It is therefore difficult to generalise. Moreover to find that the market is not ideal does not necessarily entail that public intervention will be an improvement. The net benefits or costs of government activity may well be worse than leaving the market alone. Intervention will have costs or disadvantages as well as benefits, and problems with the market may best be tackled not by direct government intervention but by the encouragement of voluntary or cooperative action, or some hybrid of the public and private sectors.

6.10 In general terms however we accept that the market is an inadequate and inappropriate device for the allocation and distribution of land and real property. There are the minimum problems of environmental amenity, of the needs of particular social groups for access to certain land uses, of the implications of development for the provision of public services, of the need to assist or supercede the market in order to assemble land for development. The presumption must be that the effects of the market have to be under constant surveillance and may in particular instances require amelioration if not modification. The belief that the market will be best under all circumstances cannot be sustained: beyond this we are agnostic.

The most appropriate level of government for town and country planning

6.11 The main disagreements here result from answering the

question: in general, should the planning system be more 'top-down' than it is now with local authorities acting simply as agents of central government, or should it be more 'bottom-up' with more policy decisions made at the local level, relatively unconstrained by central government dictate?

6.12 There are, however, a number of subsidiary questions of importance. Amongst those who favour a more 'bottom-up' approach for example, some believe that although decisions would, under such a regime, prove more democratic and accountable, enjoy the benefits associated with greater local knowledge, and offer less standardised government and therefore greater choice, they would also show a *tendency* to be more inequitable and inconsistent. In such a case therefore an important subsidiary question would be: who would arbitrate over disputes, say between local authorities at local government boundaries?

6.13 Others, in answer to this, suggest that the most efficient effective and equitable results will be assured if local authorities are allowed to bargain with one another rather than have solutions imposed from above. Yet others however, suggest that although the number of inter-authority disputes is grossly exaggerated their resolution can be best handled by an upper tier authority through the use of incentives and disincentives rather than *controls* on lower tier authorities and by adoption of the principle of 'compensation' for public 'bads'. A local authority which has to accept a development which has undesirable side effects in its area, a polluting factory, a regional airport, a costly housing estate, will receive some kind of compensation in return, such as more resources for community facilities.

6.14 In effect this latter group is suggesting that although in general they wish to advocate a more 'bottom-up' planning system, they must also allow some exceptions to the general rule. Many, for instance, argue that there are still some kinds of planning decisions which require more consistent decisions or more explicit national policy.

6.15 The sorts of decision people have in mind in this respect (and this applies equally to those favouring a more 'top-down' planning system) cover a wide range of issues: the need for and the location of nuclear power plants, defence installations, national roads, and airports; policy on inter-city public transport; the regional distribution of population and employment; and policy on the preservation and conservation of natural resources and agricultural land. The recent major inquiry at Sizewell, for example, has come under heavy criticism from those who believe central government has abrogated its responsibilities to formulate a national energy policy and that the inquiry system has been used as a substitute for deliberations which should take place within central government. Some, moreover, think there is a need for a regional form of government to make certain planning decisions over such things as public transport, hypermarkets, recreation and leisure developments in the countryside which affect urban dwellers, and the intra-regional distribution of population, employment and public utilities.

6.16   Amongst those who favour a more consistent and 'top-down' approach on the other hand, because they believe it can ensure a greater equalisation of wealth, and more efficient government, there are, equally, those who believe that more opportunities should be afforded for the local authorities to contribute to the initiation and formulation at higher levels: some decisions require a greater input at the regional, county or local level than occurs at present.

6.17   As part of this debate there is an argument which focuses on the particular role of the Planning Inspectorate and planning appeals. Some see the inquiry system purely as a check on local authority decisions to ensure that they are procedurally fair and in accordance with local wishes. Others see the inquiry system *additionally* as a check on local authority decision making to ensure that central government policy is being taken into account by local authorities when dealing with developers' proposals or the resolution of conflicts between local authorities. Yet others see the inquiry system as a check on the abuse of power by central government itself, pointing to the recent draft green belt circular as an example of what might happen if central government proceeded without reference to an outside view.

6.18   Our principal conclusion is that whatever the exact division of responsibilities for planning between central and local government (and other bodies), central government has a critical role. This is to formulate national policies to inform, guide and constrain decisions taken by local government. This central responsibility seems to us to have been neglected if not entirely abrogated. Local government has been left to initiate change and central government policy develops as a reaction to specific proposals by local authorities and others. In many instances this approach is wholly inadequate.

6.19   The vacuum at the centre and its implications for the planning system have become particularly acute in the field of energy policy. Successive public inquiries into major national developments have had to grapple with questions which are essentially ones of national policy, a process which recently culminated at Sizewell with the bizarre spectacle of teams of experts travelling from London to the salt marshes of Suffolk to dispute with each other the national demand for electricity and much else of no particular local significance. This is only an extreme symptom of a more general complaint. Central government appears to have abandoned any responsibility for the national distribution of population and employment. Many local authorities have adopted policies to encourage economic development and investment without reference to their relative employment conditions. This has been described as an 'almost endless zero-sum game of redistributing a shrinking pool of jobs'.[1] It is difficult to assess the likely effect of policies designed to attract the small and decreasing pool of footloose industry, but we question whether it is really a matter of indifference to central government whether they favour the prosperous or the depressed areas.

6.20   The same disinclination to formulate national policy, where it is clearly needed, is apparent in such matters as agricultural land protection, rural planning, nature conservation, and the coastline, minerals and aggregates. Where central government has pronounced on these issues, there have been inconsistencies between departments and much evidence of opacity and ad hockery. Numerous examples could be cited. A few will suffice. The government's attitude towards the conservation of rural and agricultural landscapes of ecological value has been most uncertain: the policies of MAFF, aimed at encouraging production, have been in direct conflict with the conservation policies of the DOE and the Countryside Commission. There has been equal uncertainty about the government's attitude to the relative merits of inner city development (and redevelopment) as opposed to the use of greenfield sites, though the Circular 14/84 on green belts represents a considerable improvement.

6.21   National policy statements should provide genuine assistance to local authorities and developers in their attempts to determine or predict the choices that should and will be made between competing uses for land. Trade-offs between different interests are inevitable, but there is little point in drawing up policy statements if they cannot help to resolve the conflicts that occur. Policy has to contain guidance as to the priority to be given to different interests. As the Scottish Development Department has put it: 'Planning Guidance at the national level must steer between unhelpful generalisations and unwelcome direction'.[2]

6.22   We are not about to advocate a national structure plan. That would be too rigid and inflexible. But we see no good reason why the approach contained in the Scottish Development Department's 'National Planning Guidelines' and 'Land Use Summary Sheets' should not be applied to the rest of the United Kingdom. This approach has the advantages of clarity, simplicity and brevity and we shall return to it below.

6.23   By contrast we are firmly of the opinion that central government has become too much involved in certain other types of decision which relate to the need for or location of particular types of land use or development, often because it has failed to make a clear distinction between advice and direction. It is difficult to see what interest is served by intervention on such matters as the location of hypermarket developments or green belts, unless it concerns the protection of prime agricultural land, or involves increased resources. There are numerous other examples of central government's interference on matters of essentially local concern, although the present government is committed to disengage itself from local planning matters. It is a question of a mistaken strategy: of trying to guide the system by detailed intervention rather than by the provision of a framework of general policy.[3]

6.24   The planning appeals system is relevant here. Along with several others, we take the view that the present appeals system combines two roles which should be kept separate. The essentially judicial function of ensuring due process and the protection of individual liberties should not be combined with the function of ensuring the correct interpretation and implementation of central government policy. The answer may be to make the Planning Inspectorate independent of the DOE and to devise a different system for applications to be 'called in' by central government in order to ensure that its policies are being taken into account by local authorities.

6.25   Finally there is the question of the structure of government below the national level. It is clear from the evidence we received that few people are happy with the present structure of local government as it affects planning and that some hanker not only after reorganisation but the creation of a regional tier of authorities. There are equally strong views about the inadequacy of the present arrangements for local government finance. We have much sympathy with these views, but have resisted the temptation to include local government reform within the remit of our recommendations. While the structure of local government is of great importance to planning, and the present structure is not in our view well adapted to its requirements, planning is only one function of local government. There would be little point in redesigning the structure of local government for the purposes of planning alone even if we disposed of the time and resources to embark on a task which has engaged and daunted a series of Royal Commissions and official inquiries. The regional dimension however is inescapable and deserves some discussion. The present government does not appear to appreciate the importance of a strategic level of planning beyond that contained in structure plans, that is at the metropolitan or supra-county levels. There are many instances where decisions are too important for the representatives of a single local authority to make alone but are not really appropriate for central government. Conflicts between neighbouring local authorities over a development at their boundaries or the location of a regional facility, such as a bus station or lorry park, which everybody needs but nobody wants, need to be resolved but do not necessarily involve issues of national policy. Local authorities may also lack the resources to provide 'regional' facilities on their own. For such issues there is a need for some kind of regional or inter-metropolitan planning. We are not convinced that this requires a separate regional tier of government. The advantages of a 'regional planning' solution based on inter-local authority bargaining seem generally to be undervalued and we shall suggest below arrangements which increase the incentives for local authorities and other public agencies to negotiate and bargain with each other as part of the planning process. It is also the case that central government is often better placed than are regional authorities for the task of equalising resources between units of local government. There will always be room for argument over the allocation of functions and responsibilities between tiers of government. No division is ideal and to create additional tiers of government may increase the difficulties of coordination and cause more confusion and delay.

We are in no doubt however about the importance of strong local planning authorities operating within a clear framework of national policy but with a greater discretion and a more ambitious conception of planning. We make suggestions as to how this might be achieved below.

The scope of the town and country planning system

6.27 The key question here is should planning be limited to pursuing objectives that relate directly to the quality of the physical environment, or should it extend to other goals as well such as unemployment, or the *ownership* of land and property. This is perhaps one of the most important areas of disagreement of all. Although many, if not most, of our contributors see planning as having a broad range of purposes and the trend has most certainly been in that general direction, there is still a hard core which wishes to see its scope much more limited. Some believe it necessary to limit planning to working for a more aesthetically pleasing, convenient, conserved and efficient physical environment, because they fear too broad a remit dissipates its effectiveness.

6.28 This is one issue where there is a real danger of over-simplifying the disagreements. The distinction between physical goals and other social and economic goals does seem particularly important, but there is a very broad range of goals with which various groups have identified and over which difficulties arise. And of course there are differences over the weighting or priority given to each goal.

6.29 We list below the more fundamental of the objectives which have appeared most frequently in our evidence, all of which have been regarded as relevant to planning. Some contributors to the Inquiry believe only a few of the list should be relevant to planning; others argue for including more or less the whole range. [These concerns are more fully described in Appendix III.] The objectives concern the impact of *site-specific* land use changes or changes to the land fabric (for example, building) on:

Environmental quality;
The physical standard of living provided (for example, its safety, health, amenity) for site users;
The capacity of publicly supplied facilities (for example, schools, sewers, roads) which 'service' sites and their use, and hence the impact on public expenditure;
The geographical mix or distribution of land uses and land fabrics;
The *need* for certain land uses and land fabrics (for example, housing, schools);
Conservation needs and good land husbandry;
The capacity of *privately* supplied facilities (for example, shops) which service sites and their use, and hence the impact on other private expenditure;
The incidence of the 'profit' associated with the change;
Economic growth, labour employment and the level of 'competition';
Community spirit;
Neighbourhood character/socio-economic composition;
The provision of public infrastructure (for example, parks, roads);
The redistribution of wealth;

Assisting property market adjustments (for example, land assembly processes);
Urban renewal.

6.30 We have already dealt above with general arguments for government intervention in land use. Here we are concerned with how far that intervention should go and how intervention in land use compares with other instruments of government policy. It is no doubt important for planning to concentrate on goals which relate directly to the quality of the physical environment. But it is clear that if planning is limited to such matters it will either not engage with what are seen to be the important questions for the future, or there will be a tendency to exaggerate the effects that improvements to the physical environment can achieve. Planning so defined would be largely irrelevant to questions such as unemployment or poor economic growth, and yet policies on land development are bound to have an important bearing on them. In fact to define the brief of planning too tightly is to deny government a valuable instrument in tackling its most urgent problems. On the one hand planning decisions would give automatic priority to environmental goals; and on the other environmental considerations would be ignored in the formation of general economic policy. Only when planning is allowed to take into account the full range of government objectives will the coordination and the trade offs necessary to coherent policy making take place. We do not accept the argument that the possibility that local planning decisions will conflict with national policies is a reason for limiting the grounds on which those decisions are made. For the fact is that a local authority pursuing the most limited environmental objectives may still frustrate central government policy, if national policy is not part of the framework in which its planning decisions are made. Local policies cannot simply be given narrow objectives: they have to incorporate broader objectives as well. This means first that there have to be clearly defined national policies; second that local authorities are obliged to have consideration for them both in plan making and in the exercise of development control; and third that central government must be able to call in applications or decisions for review where local authorities appear to be ignoring national policy. While we accept a wide brief for planning, we are not at all happy about certain reasons put forward by local authorities (and central government) to justify planning decisions. One complaint is the refusal of development applications on the grounds of the availability of public services: that to accept a particular development would impose severe pressure on the capacity of public facilities, such as schools, sewers, water supplies and roads.

107

Another concerns the prevention or lack of support for development which puts pressure on the capacity of private facilities, such as shops or sources of employment. If we regard it as legitimate to refuse planning permission for a housing development because there are not enough schools, shops or local jobs, the result will be either inertia or public monopoly in the supply of the required services. On this view 'service functions' may well be a relevant condition on a planning permission but they should not provide a reason for refusal, except where the lack of service capacity reflects a deliberate choice of policy by national government.

6.31 Some of us are also concerned by the temptation to refuse or place conditions on a planning permission when the developer appears to pay inadequate attention to internal layout and servicing on his site or to construction problems. There is a difference of opinion between those who favour the maxim 'caveat emptor' and think that the planning authority should not get involved in matters which are purely internal to the development, and those who feel that planning authorities can and do play a positive role in helping applicants to solve their siting, service and construction problems. Our general disposition however is to leave such matters to the discretion of planning authorities and let them live with the consequences of the policies they choose to pursue. It will be for them to discriminate between bad design which affects the user of a site only, such as a lack of privacy, and that which may also create problems for others, such as poor access to garages, which may result in parking on the highway, and hence to traffic hazards or to difficulties with refuse collection. And likewise for them to decide whether they should bother themselves with this sort of problem at all.

Social prescriptions

6.32 Post war planning has seen several fashions in settlement policy. The debate is a lively one although perhaps less so than it was. Support can still be found for continuing policies of urban concentration, allied to such devices as green belts, new and expanded towns and key settlements, and founded on the twin ideas of a clear division between town and country *and* an optimum size for towns. On the other hand there are people willing to advocate the removal of policies of restraint and the encouragement of a more scattered settlement system. It is argued that policies for urban concentration have only served to increase land prices in the urban areas and forced commuters to leapfrog the green belt.

6.33 There are also disagreements over whether pressures for new development or urban growth should be channelled back into the established urban areas through the rehabilitation or redevelopment of inner cities, rather than be allowed to increase the rate of loss of agricultural land. The value placed on conservation has clearly been growing. But it is possible to detect something of a backlash emerging against what has been considered by some to be stagnation. Moreover the bad memories of the redevelopment programmes of the sixties and early seventies are fading, and some people are beginning to promote the cause of redevelopment again.

6.34   Subsumed within both of these broad arguments are ones that concern whether or not land uses should be as strictly zoned as has been usual in the past—whether more mixed use developments should be allowed than before through relaxation of the non-conforming use concept. And there are arguments that relate *not* to the specific form of settlement but to the type of organisation which should be encouraged to carry out or occupy the development that takes place. This has already been touched on above in discussion of 'market attitudes', since private enterprise and private consumption are favoured by one group, while others stress the role of public agencies or the need for greater encouragement of the voluntary or cooperative sectors.

6.35   We take an agnostic view of the social prescriptions which were once confidently advocated: the political commitment to particular forms of settlement—high density, new towns, green belts, scattered development or whatever—has faded as each type of development reveals its drawbacks as well as its advantages, and no pattern seems obviously preferable to another. Planners now see that there are few unquestionable verities, no single optimal human geography. Whether or not a particular pattern is desirable or acceptable depends on local circumstances and Britain is not uniform. The absence of uniformity however is not a reason for making no prescriptions at all and most planners still see value in some of their prescriptions such as green belts, high density but not high rise, or urban containment. Others have no particular preferences and accept that there are more trade offs between one value and another than used to be assumed.

6.36   If this is indeed the case we should perhaps accept and even encourage diversity. Central government should not then attempt to impose uniformity but respect and enhance the diversity of settlement that already exists by leaving the decisions to local government.

6.37   We think the same line should be taken about decisions on the types of enterprise to be encouraged and about the relative

merits of conservation and rehabilitation as opposed to development. Flexibility is the key. In certain circumstances and places
voluntary action, the involvement of community groups, rehabilitation and conservation will prove attractive. Elsewhere the
private sector will be allowed to develop. There is no need for
central government to lay down or even encourage a standard
approach. Where grants and incentives are needed to promote
positive action, the temptation should be resisted to make one
approach much more financially viable than another.

The style and instruments of planning

6.38   The next focus of disagreement concerns procedural goals for
planning, and in particular the distinction between those who wish
to see planning as largely passive and reactive, acting to control
the initiatives of others (whether these be from the private or the
public sectors) and those who believe it should involve, in addition,
a more positive or creative role than exists at present, trying to
make desirable development take place.

6.39   This is a more general formulation of the distinction
commonly made between control or regulation on one side and
promotion on the other, but does go a little further. Some people
believe that government should keep to an essentially regulatory
role, standing back from the market and judging the initiatives
coming from that market by reference to whether or not the 'public
interest' is served. On such a view the essential role of the planning
system is to minimise the disharmony or the social costs that arise
from individual decisions about land use and development. Moreover such a role is often believed to be as far as intervention can
practically go since promotion is thought seldom to achieve its
intended effect and to produce instead undesirable side effects. But
development control as a means of implementing forward 'development plans' is often criticised for placing too heavy a reliance on
the rejection or acceptance of the applications put forward by
developers. It is thought to be especially ineffective at times of slow
economic growth, when planning cannot fall back on the luxury of
channelling development pressures where it wishes them to go.
Thus there is a need for a more positive, interventionist role for
government, promoting and championing developments of the right
kind in the right place by various means. This may mean that the
public sector should carry out development initiatives itself. At the
very least it should coordinate and manage the various inputs into
the development process from land owners, developers, public
utilities and consumers to ensure that once started the process is
carried through to successful completion. In this view planning

involves the guidance or promotion of change with a much greater emphasis on trying to shape the future or making things happen rather than waiting for them to happen.

6.40   There is little doubt that development control is that part of the planning system best understood by the general public and most readily supported. It preempts disputes between neighbours, protects public health and safety and attempts to keep the demands made on public services within a reasonable compass. Individual decisions may be contested but in general this limited and reactive style of planning is understood and accepted. To move beyond this is to multiply the difficulties. Some planning authorities, which still experience pressure for development, have used their powers to lever out of developers schemes more favourable to the public interest than they would otherwise promote. In other instances planning authorities have themselves been developers and have used their powers of acquisition and their financial resources to undertake joint enterprises with private developers or other public agencies. This more positive planning is altogether more ambitious and more controversial: it is not a matter of limiting or constraining some private benefit for the sake of a residual public interest. It is a case of creating a benefit in the public interest, which will also and inevitably be a benefit to some groups or persons more than others. It is inherently more 'political'.

6.41   It also requires more in the way of forethought and coordination: departments within local authorities must work with each other and with other public authorities, and finally they must work with central government to the extent at least of ensuring benevolent neutrality before the commitment of any substantial resources.

6.42   All this is commonplace. The problem is that it has become much more difficult to achieve over the last ten years. The planning function was split in 1974. The residual machinery for regional policy has been disbanded. Central government appears indifferent if not hostile to the idea of coordinating physical, social and economic policy in any systematic way. The modest experiments of the sixties and early seventies have run into the sand and the present political climate is inclement.

6.43   There are however good grounds for supporting a positive style of planning and the instruments necessary to implement it. The old assumption was that economic growth or development could be taken for granted and what was needed was to direct it into acceptable channels and to see that its benefits were distributed with reasonable equity. But in many parts of the

111

country stagnation and recession have long since removed any spontaneous pressure for development. Reactive planning has nothing to work on and is unable to implement the kinds of policies it once used to, let alone tackle new problems. It is for instance much less easy now to make provision for open space and other community facilities, which once were provided by the private developer. The division of the country between a prosperous south and an impoverished north is increasingly stark. This division overrides those between inner city and outer suburb, between council and private estate. In the north reactive planning simply cannot ensure minimum standards of provision, even in its relatively prosperous areas. It falls to the public sector to make good the difference at a time of increasing pressure to cut public expenditure.

6.44 Nobody would argue that we should attempt to preserve communities that are clearly in a state of terminal decline. Derelict land and an unemployed work force may well be symptoms of the inefficiency of our economic system but it can be equally or even more inefficient to prop up lame duck industries and their associated settlements. In truth we do not have any exact appreciation of the extent to which the attempt to reduce regional differences or disparities is likely to be at the expense of aggregate national well being, or even national economic growth. Policies are certainly needed to temper the harshness of decline. Equally it is necessary to make realistic assessments of the potential of our towns and cities to attract investment sufficient for our economic survival. In certain circumstances it may be necessary to encourage and even to assist the movement of vulnerable groups to areas of greater potential. The evidence suggests that labour migration is never powerful enough to overcome the disparities between regions. It is certainly the case that the social costs of labour migration, in the disruption of social ties, the destruction of communities and the abandonment of social infrastructure, are much higher than the social costs of capital migration. Within regions the problems are different and the managed decline of particular settlements may be both possible and desirable.

6.45 The case for leaving things to the market rests heavily on the argument that we do not understand enough about underlying demographic and employment trends to intervene effectively, even if we wanted to. This is a coherent, if despairing, position but one that ought not to be relied upon by any government which like the present one continues to use regional policy tools and whose decisions on its own capital investment programme have a major regional impact.

6.46   There are really two questions involved. Should government attempt to influence the distribution of population and employment? And if so, is planning a good way of attempting to do so? Our answer to the first question is yes, if it can at a reasonable cost. The answer to the second question is also yes, but the question needs to be broken down: if planning is an appropriate means of influencing the distribution of population and employment, should it aim to facilitate changes which the market is already making, should it attempt to ameliorate the bad effects of market led changes, or should it resist the lead of the market and attempt to lead the pattern of development itself? The first two of these aims are compatible with each other and acceptable to us. The third we think a legitimate ambition but one unlikely to be fulfilled save in a minority of cases, without a degree of intervention which would have political implications most of us would not welcome. Our vision of planning lies somewhere between damage control and the command economy: it should involve both steering spontaneous pressures for development into acceptable channels and encouraging development which is socially desirable though not provided by the market. It is inescapably political and cannot be confined to questions of physical amenity or conservation. For if planning does not engage with the main generators of change in our patterns of land use, it will become peripheral. Changes are taking place which have and will continue to have profound effects on the way we use our limited resources of land and the settlements we inhabit. Economic recession, the shift of manufacturing industry out of the conurbations, declining rates of population growth and the changing composition of the population, deindustrialisation and the growth of employment in the service sector, the growth of owner occupation and of car ownership: all must be taken into account by planning, and planning must involve some judgement as to the desirability of the impact such changes have on land use, and planning must have powers to influence those impacts.

6.47   We accept that the plea of ignorance is a powerful one, but think it more powerful at national than at local level. We therefore welcome the government's initiatives on simplified planning zones (SPZs) but only insofar as they add to the array of instruments available to local planning authorities. We remain to be convinced that central government does not intend to impose the idea of SPZs upon unwilling local planning authorities and that those authorities will be allowed to introduce SPZs at their own discretion. Otherwise this will prove to be yet another instance where central government interferes in what must be essentially local matters. We cannot see any national interest being served by the imposition of SPZs: the costs and benefits of any such scheme depend very much on local conditions and can only sensibly be determined by the authority on the spot. We commend the variant on the SPZ idea suggested by the Swansea Enterprise Zone, where the scheme specifies the type of development for which planning permission is granted, leaving all other development subject to normal planning controls. We agree with the Royal Town Planning Institute's contention: 'The other option of a planning scheme granting permission for any type of development apart from specific exclusions is a recipe for attracting developments that would not otherwise be welcome and whose presence might deter others'.[4] Without this condition an SPZ will threaten the security of existing owners and investors in the area affected and will fail to provide adequate protection for their environmental standards. It is equally important that an SPZ should be included as a proposal in a local plan and should be in accordance with any adopted local plan.

6.48   On the issue of compensation and betterment we believe that there would have been great advantage in maintaining the development land tax (DLT) system, with marginal changes to the rates of tax as and when appropriate. Beyond this we have not reached complete agreement. Some of us feel that this is another area where central government should disengage itself from matters of essentially local concern: there is little evidence to link land taxation to poor economic performance and central government should continue to allow and even encourage the adoption by individual local authorities of their own policies on planning gain. DLT itself was yielding an inadequate return as a result of exemptions and allowances. Others of us reject the localist case on this issue, believe that land taxation must be a national concern, think the DLT was adequate and that the returns reflected recession rather than inherent weakness in the system.

Town and country planning's democratic base

6.49   The most important choice here concerns *from whom* the principal initiative for planning should come. Who should articulate the needs and demands relevant to planning—grassroots or pressure groups (a more participative form of democracy), the professionals controlled by politicians (bureaucratic democracy) or the elected politicians themselves (representative democracy)? The choice is usually simplified to that between a stengthening of representative democracy and a greater devolution of power to grassroots organisations. But the issue of delegation of decision making power given to officials is also important.

6.50   The encouragement of public participation in planning since the Skeffington Committee reported in the late 1960s[5] has without doubt led to a valuable opening up of the planning process. The general public is now much more aware of planning issues and decisions are more in tune with public demands and needs. This reflects a strong and growing desire to 'have a say' in what happens on many fronts, on jobs and the local economy, schools, hospital services, public transport, housing and recreation. The institutions of representative democracy have offered too little opportunity for the direct involvement of members of the public in the past, and in planning, as in other areas of public policy, special public interest groups have emerged to remedy the deficiency. These developments have been uneven. Participation has been strongest on the part of those interested in preservation, the resistance to any change, and the protection of particular neighbourhoods.

6.51   Conservation, the enhancement of existing landscapes and buildings, and new development have enjoyed less organised public support and there can be little doubt that the protection of the amenities of the better off has been to date the main result of increased participation. The answer must be to extend participation, but in the end there is no substitute for an effective system of representative government, locally and nationally, in which elected representatives make decisions in the public interest and can be held accountable for them. Interest groups, local or national, are perfectly entitled to try to influence those decisions but the decisions themselves and the responsibility for them must be placed firmly with the representatives of the wider electorate. This in turn requires clearly articulated policies on the part of government and much more transparent procedures for decision making. The shortcomings of central government in these respects have become increasingly apparent with the evolution of public inquiries. We are not concerned here with the great majority of local inquiries, but with the small number of 'big public inquiries' into major developments with national policy implications. These inquiries have evolved into a new institution: an inquest of the nation rather than an occasion to ventilate grievances or resolve local disputes. The big public inquiries have become major political events: they take longer, show more concern for thoroughness and detail, involve issues which are of increasing technical complexity and are more inherently controversial, from highways to nuclear power. Their subject matter has in fact been extended as a matter of ministerial discretion (and political expediency). National policy issues have become increasingly prominent: it is not just a case of the location of a power station, but the wider implications for society of the use of nuclear power that are considered. Alternative types of investment are canvassed and objectors question the need for proposed developments whether they be airports or power stations. These considerations take inquiries far beyond issues directly concerned with land use, under pressure from objectors and with support from the courts for a wide interpretation of 'other material considerations' relevant to applications. Part cause and part consequence of these developments has been the emergence of a much more sophisticated community of objectors on issues of national policy, less disruptive than the protestors at highway inquiries in the sixties, but also requiring to be taken more seriously and not easily disfranchised by reversing the evolution of inquiries.

6.52 Inquiry procedures were not designed for the purposes to which they are now put and despite important developments they remain the subject of formidable criticism from many of those who have been involved. From the point of view of examining issues of national policy, big inquiries are held in the wrong places: Windscale or Sizewell. The wrong parties are involved: the accident of location of a national development throws a quite unfair burden on the local planning authority where the site happens to be. The inquiry uses the wrong techniques: adversarial proceedings are not the right way to sift scientific evidence on matters of great uncertainty. There is a gross imbalance of resources between the proponents and objectors, and the presumption that the proponents' case in introducing new and controversial technology stands unless objectors can upset it is wrong in itself: it should be for the proponents to prove that what they propose is necessary and reasonably safe. Such inquiries are likely to be incomplete: they depend on who chooses to object and on what grounds, with what interest, degree of skill and resources. And finally it seems to be generally agreed that such inquiries place an inordinate and unwarranted strain on all the participants: proponents, objectors and not least the inspector and his team.

6.53 There have been improvements: as one inquiry succeeds another there is a greater level of technical and professional skill all round. There were important innovations at Sizewell, in the form of preliminary meetings, the exchange of evidence in advance, the appointment of inspector's counsel to pursue matters not taken up by objectors, and the calling by the inspector of additional expert evidence. There have also been useful developments in the post inquiry phase, such as the publication of reports and parliamentary debates on them before ministerial decisions are made.

6.54 None of these improvements, nor the more radical proposals for the introduction of a two stage inquiry, go to the main point. Inquiries are used in this way because of the opportunity they present to challenge and scrutinise in detail *national* policy, and the lack of confidence in other institutions, especially Parliament, to do that job adequately. Even if inquiry procedures can be further improved it will remain a matter of chance which policies get this treatment. Mr Anthony Barker has recently proposed in a lecture to the Royal Society of Arts[6] that the inquiry system should be linked more closely into Parliament and this is a line which in present circumstances we think ought to be pursued. But no potential objector would be willing to sacrifice the present opportunity for open scrutiny of government policy through the inquiry system, however unsatisfactory, for parliamentary scrutiny of the kind given to defence or education policies. This leaves government in the position of having to live with an increasingly expensive and time consuming extra-parliamentary procedure; or of having to think of changes in parliamentary procedures which would both satisfy public expectations and be conducive to the efficient conduct of public business. There is a third option, which is to bypass planning procedures altogether where major national projects are concerned. This is what the Government has done on the Channel Tunnel, which has profound implications for land use in the immediate vicinity and beyond, none of which are to be investigated, anticipated or controlled. We have no doubt that many will have cause eventually to regret this policy of nescience.

Town and country planning's institutional form

6.55 Under this heading the main division occurs between those who believe that the principal responsibility for planning should lie with those authorities which are charged with general governmental responsibilities for an area (elected local authorities) and those who advocate more use of special functional agencies (on the assumption that these will generally be non-elected or at least indirectly elected, like urban development corporations, development agencies, the Countryside Commission). The suggestion is usually that the specialised agencies tend to be more efficient and effective, but that this has to be traded off against the problems of accountability they may pose.

6.56 There is wide support for much better coordination between and also within government agencies, largely in order to ensure that fewer conflicting proposals are carried forward. Many contributors to the Inquiry have pointed to planning issues over which integration is lamentable or even entirely lacking. The commonest proposals to improve coordination rely first of all upon asserting an integrating role for some government agency further up the hierarchy, and then on removing responsibility for matters over which there is any genuine conflict to that agency. Few contributors to the Committee's discussions have offered much support for a more 'competitive' and pluralistic public sector, in which a network of government agencies has overlapping, concurrent, jurisdictions and functions, and each negotiates with the others but from the standpoint of a particular interest. The end result would be a negotiated rather than imposed order when conflicts do arise.

6.57   Our earlier comments on the need for positive promotional and interventionist planning in times of recession imply a willingness to experiment with instruments and institutions which will facilitate it. We have already expressed some suspicion of non elected special purpose agencies. Our reservations however extend only insofar as these agencies are allowed or obliged to make controversial decisions in the absence of public discussion. As administrative agencies given the task of implementing planning proposals which have been subject to public inspection and political debate, we can see that special purpose agencies have numerous advantages. The Scottish Development Agency (SDA) appears to be much more successful in this respect than the Docklands Development Corporation, in part perhaps because the SDA places much more emphasis on the mobilisation of public and political support for its programme.

6.58   Coordination of physical planning with other forms of planning is commonly advocated. It is much less often practised. The division of labour between professions and institutions is necessary and because it is necessary becomes so ingrained that extraordinary efforts are needed to overcome its disadvantages. While a specialist agency may be able to overcome professional differences and combine professional skills in pursuit of certain limited aims, there remains a wider problem of effecting co-ordination between institutions or departments which continue to maintain their separate identities. On this count we find the government's retreat from the regional report system in Scotland surprising. That approach to the coordination of local government planning had a great deal to commend it and we think that it ought not only to be reinstated in Scotland but to be given much wider application.

The professional function

6.59   The debate over planning has long included a largely unresolved discussion of whether the planning professional should be a specialist or generalist. To some, perhaps a majority, planning is largely about formulating and implementing proposals for the development of land; it focuses on building and other physical changes to the built and 'natural' environment and the use to which land is put. It is seen largely as a means to other much more fundamental ends rather than an end in itself (though some even see it as that); the basic rationale generally offered is the failure of market forces and processes on their own to provide a satisfactory physical environment for living, working and recreation. On this view there is generally an acceptance of the need for some effort to be put into coordinating planning in one government agency with that in another, and at coordinating planning with other forms of governmental activity which may be seeking to achieve similar goals, especially other departments and agencies involved in land development and the physical environment such as housing, environmental health and transport departments and development agencies. But this integration is not an overriding concern.

6.60 To the generalists, however, coordination is the central concern of planning. Planning is about integrating all the policy making and implementation activities in a particular governmental body which are relevant to a particular area. There is a less extreme position—some seem to see planning as narrower than the generalist coordinated planning but broader than physical planning. Indeed we get the feeling that, for some, planning is everything a local authority does that is not happily housed in any of the other established local authority departments. Quite a few see planning as gap filling, taking on new functions as local government has been obliged to tackle new problems in new ways. And this has perhaps been one of the strengths of planning in the past. Those trained in 'traditional' planning have moved on to many new and different tasks. There are several reasons why this has been possible: because planning's original statutory powers were widely drawn; because planners have had a record of forward looking research and innovation and have never had a strong attachment to, or identification with, the administration of a particular function or service; and because planning has had a perhaps stronger problem solving orientation than other local government professional activities and has long recognised the value of coordination in problem solving.

6.61 To the generalist, planning may also involve coordinating the various policies of different government bodies and private agencies that relate to a particular area. The essence of the approach is to see planning as a means through which a local authority or a community decides on and attempts to influence its own future—

and not just its physical or land use future. 'The management of change' is the typical phrase.

6.62 There seem to us to be three not necessarily incompatible roles for the planner. First as the administrator and interpreter of a particular body of legislation (the priest of the statute); second as an expert adviser on the consequences of decisions concerned with and affecting land use and settlement patterns: this requires a deep but also broad understanding of the economic and social forces shaping our society, as well as an appreciation of the design of physical structures themselves. The planner is not of course the only professional involved in the planning process: there are also engineers, architects, surveyors and so forth. What distinguishes the planner is that he is the generalist: he has to bring together the contributions of others both to produce coherent advice on policy and to see that something happens. In this role the planner is not the master of anything: he is a visionary or a fixer. Either way he is concerned with the implications of decisions made by others: he has to steer the actions of others towards some common goal. The first role may require a straightforward professional training: the second and third require a good deal more. We have not explored how far the present education of planners fits them for these roles, but we are inclined to think that the capacity to undertake the third role is much more likely to be a matter of political education on the job, than of formal instruction. We think John Friend's description of this role as 'responsible scheming'[7] is apt and not to be despised, since it recognises the interstitial or bargaining character of much of the planner's work and its political context.

The clients of planning

6.63 To the majority of contributors to the Inquiry, the sole client of the planning 'professional' is evidently the governmental agency which pays his salary. There are quite clearly, however, other roles which planning professionals can take on. Some roles are complementary to the traditional role and others potentially contradictory. For example some planners are needed who, although employed by a government agency, will fulfil the essentially separate role of acting as intermediaries between this agency and the 'public'. In this instance the professional might best be thought of as a 'commissionaire' establishing what members of the public want in their dealings with the agency and then directing them to the department most relevant to their particular need. Another group argues that the two roles of bureaucrat and commissionaire have to be combined if only because staff resources are limited, in which case the professional may best be described as a 'gatekeeper' encouraging members of the public to seek access to a government agency but not always allowing them in. This role may well be a necessary one but clearly it can involve the professional in conflicts of interest and divided loyalties.

6.64   In consequence a final group supports the notion that the real client of at least one section of professional planners should be the public itself—which may be an individual or the public in general. Here the professional is viewed as someone who should be an 'advocate' of the public's interests, at times risking the agency's displeasure, especially when an employee. It is for this reason that some contributors have argued for a separate planning aid service.

6.65   We do not see why planners should be trained in a single mould. Planners can serve different clients: local authorities, developers, interest groups, community organisations and others. The problems arise when the planner is asked to serve more than one client at a time. The role of gatekeeper, for example, is fraught with difficulties: the attempt to combine work for a local authority and members of the public, whose interests frequently conflict, involves a high risk of forfeiting the trust of both sides.

6.66   It seems to us that there are three professional roles for the planner related to distinct client groups. First the official working for central or local government, whose job is to advise politicians and to implement their decisions. Second there is the commissionaire or access professional, dealing with members of the public on behalf of the authority and attempting to resolve conflicts on the authority's terms. And finally there is the planning advocate not only working on behalf of private and community groups, but encouraging their formation and participation in the planning process. These roles should be, and be seen to be, separate and for this to be possible public funds may need to be made available to set up planning advice services: some of the money currently spent on the 'commissionaires' might well be diverted to support outright advocates, perhaps through the medium of community groups. Again we have not explored this matter in detail, but we think that it should be question of local discretion and that any obstacles to the exercise of such discretion should be removed.

6.67   We have so far discussed the profession as if it were a single body wholly concerned with working for government. In fact there are in the private sector not only 'self made' planners, such as the owners of large estates or the private developers with their shopping centres, industrial estates and new towns, but other professionals, such as land agents, chartered engineers and particularly chartered surveyors. These professionals may be said to be involved in 'privatised' planning and since there may in the future be much more reliance placed on this sort of planning, their training skills and standards are likely to be of comparable importance to those of their public sector colleagues.

Time scale in town and country planning

6.68 The very word 'planning' implies some orientation towards the future. To some, however, the fact that buildings survive for several years, yielding a stream of benefits or services over time is sufficient for the process of making decisions dealing with land and buildings to be called 'planning'. Whether planning is 'short term' or 'long term' depends on the number of years the environmental costs and benefits of the change are thought certain enough to incorporate in the decision. And in such instances what is thought to be required is some assessment of the merits of a new proposal in relation to a set of minimum standards agreed upon at the present time.

6.69 A second view of planning involves deciding at one point in time the criteria which will be used in making development decisions for the next, say, ten years. At the end of the period a reassessment of the criteria, and hence of the plan, can take place. In this case planning may be considered short or long term depending on the frequency of plan review.

6.70 To yet another group, a more specific meaning is reserved for the word 'planning' and this governs its whole approach to what form of planning is desirable: planning is about deciding what constitutes a desirable future in, say, ten years, working towards that target, predicting the future, estimating problems and opportunities over the span of years that might arise for the plan's implementation, and proposing a programme of contingent decisions that will need to be made over that time in order to achieve the plan. In essence this notion of 'planning' involves deciding on the future, predicting and then making choices on the decisions that will be required at various points up to that future in order to ensure its outcome. Any form of decision making which fails to incorporate these basic ingredients should not be labelled 'planning'. For this group planning can be either short term or long term depending upon the number of years for which a schedule or programme of decisions is drawn up, the distance into the future which the 'plan' represents.

6.71 Under all these approaches, it should be clear, planning can be seen as an iterative process, requiring monitoring and review of 'plans'. Planning can also be 'flexible', adapting to change as and when necessary. And virtually everyone supports both of these notions. Under the second approach, for example, flexibility is often interpreted as meaning that each step should be sufficient in itself, should not close down too many options, and so should be capable of being stopped and altered or redirected at virtually any time.

6.72 There has been a steady shortening of the time scale considered appropriate for planning. John Friend in the essay quoted above relates this to a change in the 'traditions' which have been accepted as models of what planning should be about. The first of these was the 'project planning tradition' derived from the construction industry, production engineering and civil engineering. This tradition arises from the concerns of people charged with bringing to completion projects that call for the coordination of many interrelated activities, each of finite duration. These projects are usually thought of in terms of a particular product which has been designed and agreed in advance: an architectural design for a building, an engineering design for a new production line, a master plan for a new town. The time dimension in project planning is conceived in terms of the ordering of multiple activities in such a way as to contribute towards the completion of the project within a given time scale: the completion date is the important long term horizon on which to focus. The influence of this idea of planning appears to have been strong in the forties in the special circumstances of post war reconstruction, when the new statutory development plans were seen not only as a framework for development control but as a point of departure for ambitious public investment programmes in housing, factories, schools and roads, and all the other services associated with the development of balanced communities.

6.73 As the management of major infrastructure projects ceased to be the dominant activity of local planning authorities, planners found themselves faced with more subtle problems of trying to intervene in the activities of others, in arenas where power was often widely diffused among many different public and private organisations. In these circumstances, a systems model drawn loosely from systems engineering or cybernetics became more attractive and had considerable influence both on the advocacy of corporate planning in local government generally and on the conception of town and country planning. But for both corporate and land use planning, the systems model ran into difficulties largely because of implicit assumptions about the degree of influence that could be realistically asserted over the system from a single position of central authority. Corporate planning proved more difficult to introduce into a local authority than an industrial firm, partly because it was seen as an attempt to bypass party political competition for control and partly because of the crucial external accountability of chief officers to different departments of central government such as education, transport and health and social security. The administrative reforms of the early seventies— the reorganisation of local government to create two tiers of authority throughout the country, and the formation of new health and water authorities—meant that there were now four separate public authorities responsible for the provision of key services and the promotion of cápital projects in any particular area, and made the shortcomings of the 'central guidance' model of systems planning all the more apparent. Constraints on public expenditure were also becoming more and more severe; and the outcome seems to have been that town and country planners and corporate planning staffs alike have had to abandon most of the more grandiose ideas of the systems planning approach, and to settle for 'implementation' through whatever means of influence comes to hand.

6.74 Whether the pragmatic and bargaining style of planning which has emerged from the collapse of the project and systems models itself deserves to be dignified with the term model may be a moot point. It is certainly much closer to the planners' experience of operating development control. It conceives planning essentially as a publicly accountable way of dealing with localised tensions or conflicts between the claims of different parties over the development and use of land. The role of planners is to work between systems rather than to attempt to exercise central guidance of a single system. The planner is no longer concerned to fulfil a particular blueprint within a given time nor to steer a single system towards a clearly defined goal. His time scale is not dictated by the nature of the project nor by some imagined future for the system as a whole. Responding to problems as they arise may suggest a short time scale for planning, but in fact the time scales are necessarily various and depend on the nature of the problem with which the planner is trying to deal. Urgent pressures for decision on particular planning applications may raise questions about all kinds of other related decisions—some specific, others with a wider policy significance, some of them due to be addressed soon, others less immediate. Where the issue concerns a major investment proposal in a field such as airport siting, power generation or major road building, the decision to be made, however urgent, may itself have to be evaluated for long term repercussions of great complexity. It remains a critical function of the planner to think long about the implications of current decisions for the future freedom of action of those responsible for making them and to spell out the opportunities which may be opened up or foreclosed. A plan on this definition is a forecast of the consequences of current policies as well as a statement of what the planning authority is trying to achieve. Such plans require continual revision both because of the difficulty of predicting the outcomes of policies and changes in the external factors which influence their success or failure and because of changes of view about what is desirable on the part of the planning authority itself and on the part of the many other actors whose behaviour it is trying to influence. A short cycle of revision does not imply a short time scale for planning: it is simply an acknowledgement of the inherent uncertainty and complexity with which planners have to deal. A clear interim statement is a better guide to the planning authority itself and to those who have to do busines with it, than a long term or strategic plan which has become obsolete before even it is approved. Though it is an important function of planning authorities to provide a degree of continuity and stability, it does no service to themselves or others to pretend a degree of certainty that cannot be sustained.

6.75 There is one further aspect of time scale which deserves mention and that is related not so much to the problems with which planners have to deal as to the procedures by which they deal with them. We have already referred and shall return to the interminable procedures for the approval of structure plans. These have done much to undermine the anticipated benefits of introducing them. There is equally strong criticism of delays in the making of decisions on planning applications. Here the problem is not one of undue elaboration and detail, but of indifference to the effects of delay on the concerns of others. There is an onus on those responsible for these procedures to make sure that they are completed with despatch as the present government has forcibly and successfully urged. There is an equal onus on anybody who proposes new procedures to recognise how difficult it is to stick to timetables and how often those recommended in the past have proved utterly unrealistic. The question must never be simply whether something is worth doing, but whether it will have been worth doing by the time it is actually done. We have had this much in mind in considering our own recommendations.

Geographical variation in the planning system

6.76 Until this point we have assumed that the planning system itself—the legal and administrative framework for planning— should have the same structure across the whole country. A few contributors, however, have argued either that the present system is not uniform but should be, or else that greater geographical variation should indeed be introduced. The examples used relate to urban and rural differences, inner and outer city contrasts, and intraregional variations in the planning system.

6.77 There are strong advocates of extending the development control system to apply more completely to rural areas, and for the introduction of comprehensive planning controls over agricultural developments.

6.78 Some have called for greater experimentation with the kind of approach to planning exemplified by the enterprise zone. Equally, others support the retention of (or even further moves towards) a uniform national system of planning legislation, arguing that the localisation of legal and administrative systems can only increase complexity and uncertainty.

6.79 The 1947 Town & Country Planning Act saw as the essential task of planning the need to foresee and control the development of towns and cities. The countryside required protection from the incursion of housing and industry: that is from almost any development which clashed with the interests of agriculture. For the rest the countryside could be left to the care of its natural protectors, the farmers.

6.80 There are several reasons why this assumption has proved too simple and too sanguine. There were first the legitimate competing demands for space—for mining, motorways, airports, chemical plants, power stations and so forth—which could not be resisted. These demands apart, the rural areas if they were to retain economic and social vitality required replacement for the jobs lost through the contraction of employment in agriculture. Alternative industrial development was too often prevented in the name of good planning but more truthfuly in the interest of maintaining a monopoly for agriculture. A more important challenge has come from those concerned with recreation and conservation whose efforts have resulted in the creation of the national parks and a variety of conservation measures, culminating in the Wildlife and Countryside Act 1981. Despite these measures and more voluntary conservation undertaken by farmers themselves, the public image of the farmer has changed from benevolent caretaker to destroyer of the traditional landscape, rooting up hedgerows, cutting down immemorial oaks, spraying wildlife to death, and ploughing up land of marginal economic but great scientific value. Efforts to control this rapacious caricature have given scant satisfaction to his critics and some as we have seen would like to see agriculture brought fully within the system of development control.

126

6.81   A contrary argument has been put to us in evidence that agricultural changes are of an intrinsically different level to changes in urban land use and require a different planning approach. The extension of development control to agricultural operations would probably be ineffective: what are involved are changes in the way land is managed rather than developed and these would not be easy to influence by planning controls or conditions. Hedgerow neglect, for example, would be extremely difficult to halt by the mere application of planning permission and conditions. And a hedge once removed would often be difficult to reinstate. In such cases there is a stronger case for promotion, advice, management and incentives for conservation than for regulation.

6.82   We think there is force in this case, particularly in the light of the rapidly changing pattern of incentives for agricultural production. Policies aimed to prevent the neglect of buildings and to enforce the restoration of mineral workings which rely on normal planning controls have had little effect, and even in the urban areas there is no general form of control on the demolition of buildings or environmental features. This argument can be over-stated. The weakness of enforcement powers in urban planning is something to be rectified rather than imitated and should not be pleaded in mitigation. There are moreover problems with the alternatives to regulation which are usually advocated—namely incentives and management agreements. Their emphasis is to forestall undesirable changes rather than to encourage change for the better and incentives not to do things can have unfortunate effects: unscrupulous farmers are reputed to have blackmailed the government into paying them to desist from ploughing up or draining protected land, which they otherwise would not have considered doing. Again incentives are not necessarily adequate to prevent farmers from destroying landscape features because they want to change their land over to much more profitable urban uses.

6.83   A final argument against the introduction of planning controls over agricultural operations is that on the whole farmers can and should be trusted to manage the countryside on behalf of everyone else, and that the goodwill of the farming community is the most critical condition for the success of conservation policies. Again we see the force of this argument, though it has to be said that the majority are not the problem. The main difficulty lies with a small number of landowners whose actions have a dis-proportionate effect. The question is whether the introduction of controls to deal with a minority will alienate the majority and undo

the valuable work of persuasion upon which voluntary conservation bodies have embarked. We are certainly in favour of the
extension of development control to certain limited changes of land
use. Whether they should be extended across the board to all
farming operations we doubt. It may be as well to wait to see how
the sea change in production subsidies affects the behaviour of
farmers before abandoning the voluntary route.

Conclusion

6.84   We have now outlined the main causes of disagreement and
commented briefly upon them. Before proceeding to develop our
own views, we set out in the next chapter seven conceptions of the
proper role of planning which emerge from the multiplicity of
disagreements considered here.

Notes:

1   Royal Town Planning Institute Study Group 'The Planning Response to
    Social and Economic Change', *The Planner*, Oct. 1984, p 9
2   SDD National Planning Guidelines, Scottish Development Department
    1981, p 2
3   A strategy whose consequences are examined in detail by Patsy Healey
    in 'The Role of Development Plans in the British Planning System: An
    Empirical Assessment', in *Urban Law & Policy* (forthcoming)
4   Royal Town Planning Institute *Simplified Planning Zones*, 1984, p 9
5   *People and Planning,* Ministry of Housing and Local Government 1969
    (HMSO, London)
6   Anthony Barker 'Planning Inquiries: A Role for Parliament', *Journal of
    the Royal Society of Arts,* August 1984
7   John Friend *The Essence of Planning: Three Perspectives Compared,*
    Tavistock Institute of Human Relations, January 1985, p 16

Chapter 7   Seven Characters in Search of a System

7.1   A variety of views has been expressed on each of the dimensions of disagreement we have identified. There is therefore in theory a large number of possible combinations of views. But on inspection we have found that there is a limited number of more or less coherent 'sets' which appear to cover both the majority of issues and the majority of those expressing opinions on them. It must be said that what differentiates one set from another is not so much outright disagreement on particular issues, though that is certainly present, as differences of priority or emphasis on particular objectives. The seven positions we have identified are inevitably caricatures, that is attempts to simplify a complex situation in order to reveal its peculiar features. Nobody likes to be put in a cartoon, but we hope that our caricatures are sufficiently recognisable to illustrate the important differences between the various views of planning and their implications. Our seven 'characters' are as follows:

> The Private Developer
> The Public Developer
> The Conservationist
> The Environmentalist
> The Corporatist
> The Community Developer
> The Compleat Planner

The Private Developer

7.2   The Private Developer is generally to be found in the development industry, but his views also seem to find favour with members of Her Majesty's Government. At heart he has a basic optimism about the essential efficiency and desirability of the *market* in determining the main thrust of land use and land development. This is allied to a belief in the efficacy of using taxation and social security to tackle the problem of poverty and to ensure a fair distribution of resources, income and wealth.

7.3   Planning's main purpose is, accordingly, to protect environmental amenity and to avoid gross environmental damage. It should concentrate on a reactive response to the development initiatives of the private sector (public sector developers are generally assumed to behave—or at least to be persuadable by planners to behave—in the public interest). Controls should be limited to instances of clear necessity—indeed a streamlined form of development control like that in the simplified planning zone (SPZ) proposals would in most cases be acceptable.

7.4   The Private Developer wishes to restrict as far as possible the exercise of discretion by planning authorities in order to increase the certainty within which the development industry operates. He also wants to reduce the average length of time taken for discretionary cogitation by planning authorities. He thus favours formal 'plans' and policy statements, kept up to date, but wants to restrict the length of time taken to prepare plans (or at least the time when the standing of plans is in 'limbo'). He also wishes to restrict the importance of the 'other material considerations' component of development control decisions.

7.5   He emphasises the importance of environmental quality but is also clear that this objective can never be absolute—that environmental quality may be traded off against other, perhaps more important goals. Employment generation and the continued profitability of the development industry are examples. This trading off needs to be in the hands of central government through its call-in power. If local planning authorities are given powers to accept development applications on non environmental grounds, they might also be tempted to use these grounds to refuse applications—which would take them well beyond the realm of environmental quality protection and which would therefore be undesirable.

7.6   Very occasionally the Private Developer sees the necessity to substitute incentives for controls and also to experiment with special purpose functional agencies, like the urban development corporations, where positive public sector involvement is required. In general, however, the priority is for a *market-led* pattern of development. Positive intervention should only be used where development demand is particularly weak and would not normally be considered a part of planning.

7.7   Strategic issues such as the location of regional public facilities would in general be reserved for central government decision outside the planning system altogether. And central government would also have a role in curbing over-mighty subordinate authorities, suspending or even superceding local powers. Some Private Developers might also call in central government to curb the over-mighty developer and to prevent distortion of the market, though advocates of the market seem in practice less worried by private monopoly than by public intervention.

7.8   All in all the emphasis of the Private Developer is on a 'supply-side' economics of the development process, and the implementation of planning policies by a reactive but less cumbersome and obstructive system of development control, working to reduce instances of gross environmental damage.

The Public Developer

7.9   For the Public Developer local planning authorities should use their powers, not substantially altered from those available at present, to encourage and enable land development to take place. The defining feature is an acceptance of the basic strength and desirability of the market in determining land use and land development, coupled with a willingness to make that market work more efficiently, by 'managing' the development process. The emphasis is on positive, proactive, 'getting things done' intervention. All unnecessary obstacles to the development process, and in particular any time consuming administrative procedures involved in obtaining the various consents required before development can commence (planning permission, building regulations approval, etc), would be firmly discouraged.

7.10   Where the demand for development is not buoyant the Public Developer advocates free use of government grants and other financial incentives for Private Developers and land users to assure a sufficient level of profitability for the private sector. The application of compulsory purchase powers is approved in order to free up market processes—for example to encourage the release of land held by recalcitrant landowners holding out for excessive profits. Indeed, the Public Developer is deeply pessimistic about any reliance on spontaneous development.

7.11   In areas of high development pressure on the other hand the Public Developer would be somewhat less interventionist but even here would attempt to manage, persuade, and cajole the development industry rather than simply 'control' it. The traditional role of the planner as an umpire, adjudicating between competing interests without any influence over which interests are represented, is thought quite inappropriate for the modern world.

7.12   An important aim would be to speed up adjustment processes in the market, to bring the supply and demand for development into equilibrium. This pursuit of development, of change, rebuilding and redevelopment, is supported in order to ensure that development of the right kind occurs in the right places and at the right times. But on the whole change of this kind is considered desirable for its own sake. The Public Developer stresses the needs of industry, commerce, the development industry and 'planning for production', in the belief that the market generally knows best what people want, and that the market is the best way of ensuring people get what they want. There is a clearly perceived association between a thriving development industry and progress, employment creation and local economic growth.

7.13 The Public Developer places much less emphasis on environmental quality than the Private Developer, though this does not imply a complete neglect of environmental quality. Indeed, there is an underlying belief that a thriving development industry is likely to produce its own environmental quality. Modern factories, offices and other workplaces, modern housing and modern recreation facilities, he believes, carry their own demands for an attractive physical environment. Appreciation of the importance of satisfactory environmental conditions for work and residence is now much more likely to be built into the calculations of private developers than has ever been the case in the past. Now of course the Public Developer accepts that some environmental problems can occur. But in urban areas, in particular, the danger where development demand is buoyant is thought to be much less of a problem than it used to be: most environmental degradation occurs where demand is weak. Planning should therefore attempt to *create* the preconditions necessary for the smooth running and profitability of the development industry.

7.14 Implicit in this approach is a much more 'competitive' system of local government than we have been used to. Local authorities are expected to compete with one another to attract development, employers and residents, and to specialise in types of development where they have a comparative advantage over other local authorities. The Public Developer questions the value of a 'coordinated' approach to planning, imposed from above with little genuine autonomy for local government. It has too often stultified initiative and variety in local government and hence impeded its ability to react to new problems and situations as they arise.

The Conservationist

7.15 The Conservationist gives priority to policies and plans which *protect* the built environment, particular social environments, and, more especially, the natural physical environment. There is an emphasis on 'resource planning' since he seeks to ensure that best use is made of both the manmade and the 'natural' resources which society has inherited and acquired. In consequence there is an automatic presumption against certain types of land use or building proposal:

(i) Those which would seriously close down future options for the use of particular parcels of land (for example, where a 'needed' development can only begin some time in the future because of resource constraints or because of the difficulties encountered in assembling a 'complete' site at one time); and

(ii) Those which might lead to the destruction or sterilisation of land and local ecological habitats and, especially, to the depletion or damage of non-renewable physical and social resources such as high quality agricultural land, heritage landscapes and buildings, neighbourhood 'communities'.

Physical and social resources are thus treated as potentially finite and depletable, not infinite.

7.16 The Conservationist places his accent not on current demands but on likely *future* needs and the heritage which society passes on to its heirs. Protection of rural landscapes, old buildings, the coastline and traditional community styles of living, is considered paramount. But supporters of this approach are clear in their distinction between preservation and conservation. The former implies the fossilisation of resources as if in a museum, whereas conservation incorporates a much more active management, protection, and even enhancement, of the fixed resource base.

7.17 Environmental and ecological 'impact' assessments are considered vital if the Conservationist's approach is to prove successful. For without the necessary investment to ensure well informed decisions mistakes can easily be made. Moreover the destruction of existing habitats, environments and communities tends to receive more attention than does the creation or provision of new ones. Implicit in all this is the assumption that good physical and social environments generally come about more by good fortune than by judgement and hence every effort should be made to protect them.

7.18 In general the Conservationist believes that his policy would require a high degree of local government input, since local authorities alone can have the requisite quality and quantity of information about the potential impact of developments to make good decisions. Central government, with its emphasis on policy and on principles, is thought to be too far removed from actual, vulnerable, resources to assess the importance of particular changes or proposals. Nevertheless a more rigorous attempt to coordinate the various government agencies is often seen to be vital. Lack of communication between the various parts of the public sector is recognised to be an important cause of environmental degradation. Public agencies are often set up to achieve specific functions but with no obligation to consider the wider 'public interest'. They have little incentive to ensure the maintenance of environmental quality, and are thus a particular threat to the survival of environmental resources.

The Environmentalist

7.19   For the Environmentalist, planning should provide the means for a participating public to establish control over its own local physical environment. Planning decisions should reflect the wishes of concerned citizens to control the quality of the environment (both built and natural), within which they live and work. They should not be the result of initiatives made by individuals acting according to their own private interests and, especially, not the result of decisions made by interests external to the local community.

7.20   The issues considered important by the Environmentalist are raised both under planning legislation and under legislation on highways, housing, public health, parks and open spaces, pollution control, water authorities, factories, agriculture and the countryside. Even these legal arrangements would need to be broadened and modified however. The Environmentalist requires extensive powers concentrating on negative 'control' but also a restricted number of 'positive' powers for use in appropriate circumstances, for instance to enforce the compliance of defiant developers to the agreed environmental plan. In particular he would extend the powers which planning authorities have to police and enforce planning control decisions in order to ensure that developers do apply for planning permission when they should and do abide by planning application decisions such as refusals of and conditions on permission. The Environmentalist would increase the resources available for the surveillance of environmental changes. And he would increase the powers and resources available for modifying existing planning permissions in instances where inferior past planning decisions or subsequent on-site changes result in environmental damage. Indeed there is some encouragement for greater controls or powers relating to the control of demolition and for better powers and resources to combat dereliction and inadequate maintenance by the owners of land and buildings.

7.21 The Environmentalist advocates a participatory style of planning with initiative for planning decisions coming from citizens, perhaps channelled through neighbourhood councils, which would be given environmental powers to use in ways demanded by the community. Decisions would be made on the basis of environmental quality, but it would have to be recognised that such decisions could have non environmental impacts—and that environmental quality might have to be traded off against, for instance, the needs of employment. Indeed, different communities would probably place different weight on environmental quality at the expense of other ends. At least in this way each community would become responsible for the decisions that affect it, including the failures, rather than having them imposed from outside.

7.22 Planning appeals, against refusal of permission for instance, and arbitration over inter-neighbourhood disputes would be heard by a regional or countywide authority or at least by a body which was independent both of the local planning authority and of central government. The merits of policy would not be questioned at appeal inquiries—only the manner of its implementation. 'Call-in' powers to central government would be allowed, both of planning applications and, additionally, of positive actions by local planning authorities such as discontinuance orders. But their use would be reserved for instances where established national policies were involved. Inquiries on called-in cases would be entirely separate from the appeal process and remaining environmental controls would be transferred to the local authorities.

7.23 In short, the whole emphasis of the Environmentalist would be on local 'community self management' and on environmental quality.

The Corporatist

7.24 For the corporatist the emphasis is first and foremost on *coordinating* the various forms of government intervention—and in particular on coordinating environmental and physical planning with social, economic and resource planning. Coordination moreover would take place both within and *between* each tier of government—local, regional and national. Thus the need is stressed for formal mechanisms and procedures that will bring together at the local level the plans of district and county councils, statutory undertakers and ad hoc bodies like development corporations, alongside mechanisms for bringing together local authorities and central government.

7.25   Secondly, the emphasis is on achieving a continual, cyclical, process of plan formulation and implementation, where planning proposals are regularly monitored, evaluated, reviewed and improved—rather than on a style of planning which concentrates on producing and putting into practice blueprints for the future.

7.26   The approach of the Corporatist is hierarchical and allocative, controlled from the top. Local authorities should be able to make discretionary decisions only on matters referred to them by upper tier authorities. Provision is allowed for negotiation and bargaining between upper and lower tiers of government before a final decision is made at each round in the planning process, and so some feedback of the views of lower tiers to upper tiers is permitted and possibly even encouraged. Moreover, lower tier authorities are not seen simply as the administrative arms of central government. They will have discretionary authority which will change over time, as the upper tier authorities decide on and define what constitutes the national (or regional) interest. Nevertheless, the Corporatist approach is fundamentally organised from the top downwards and the freedom of action of local government is strictly circumscribed by central and regional government. As such it is in notable contrast to the approach advocated by the Public Developer discussed earlier, which grants local authorities a certain autonomy and a role and discretionary authority not delineated entirely by what central government will permit.

7.27   Public participation and the participation of private sector interests (commercial, industrial, development and trade union) in the planning process is very much a part of the corporatist model. Stress is placed on the partnership between governmental and private sector agencies and on a dual structure of interest groups and traditional elected bodies, which have the final word. However, participation would be strictly timetabled to accord with the planning cycle and would be restricted to matters of plan formulation and review. Participation would be less necessary and would not be encouraged at the stage of implementation. In part this may be seen as a reaction to criticism of the slow pace of planning in the past and the consequent delays and uncertainty imposed on the development process. It is argued that participation would have to fit in with the requirements of an efficient planning system. Indeed the Corporatist places much emphasis on time-tabling, regularity of procedures and quickness of response.

7.28   A typical 'planning' process might run like this:

(i) Central government instigates the formulation of a national corporate plan to be issued say, triennially or biennially. Discussions with commercial and trade union interests and lower tier authorities are set in motion;

(ii) Once central government's corporate plan is approved local authorities then immediately formulate their own corporate plans, linking land use planning with other planning. Co-ordination with other government agencies having local impacts and with commercial and trade union interests is effected;

(iii) A biennial/triennial review procedure is launched and the production of plan revisions accomplished at each cycle.

The 'plans' could start off simply and selectively, becoming more complicated and comprehensive with each new cycle of review. Particular parts of the plans rather than entire plans could be reviewed in each new cycle. Plan presentation would however concentrate on producing a more streamlined, simpler, briefer planning document than occurs presently.

7.29   The Corporatist generally favours the setting of universalistic, national minimum standards in relation to the provision of government services and public facilities, including the services and facilities in the land use and environmental planning field. There is, however, some support for regional corporate planning. Usually the regional element takes the form of proposals for non-elected regional planning councils, producing and influencing the implementation of regional corporate plans. Councils would be made up of nominated representatives from both central and local government and from relevant ad hoc government agencies (for example, development corporations, development agencies) and serviced by a minimal regional civil service. In addition they would have minimal executive functions, relying for the implementation of their proposals on the influence their plans would afford and on an ability to call upon central government assistance with recalcitrant and obstructive lower tier authorities. In this sense, and because of the hierarchial emphasis of the corporatist approach, the regional councils would be more the arms of central government than the representatives of the local authorities.

7.30   Finally, there is little doubt that the Corporatist generally favours the use of elected (albeit, in the regional council case, indirectly elected) multi-purpose government authorities rather than non-elected functional agencies, at each tier in the government hierarchy. Coordination and a reduction in the extent of shared or concurrent functions, both desirable in themselves, are thereby thought to be easier to achieve.

The Community Developer

7.31   The Community Developer emphasises that traditional town and country planning powers should be used in conjunction with other local authority powers and resources to tackle in a coherent fashion the major problems facing particular local communities. He suggests in addition that these powers and resources should be used by the local communities to meet problems and goals they themselves perceive as important. Thus the Community Developer wants to grapple with such problems as high unemployment levels and urban decay in particular local communities and so goes much further than the pursuit of environmental quality alone. Moreover he supports the view that the impetus for problem solving should come from within the local community rather than from outside it. But whilst his objectives may be in broad sympathy with those followed by the Corporatist, he goes about the achievement of these objectives in different ways, and whilst his approach to local community action is in broad agreement with the Environmentalist he pursues different objectives.

7.32   Emphasis is placed first of all on stimulating local community action, and especially action by the voluntary sector, by way of grass roots initiatives such as 'community businesses'. Financial incentives but also direct local authority development are therefore harnessed to resolve local community problems through the encouragement they can give to community 'development'.

7.33   Secondly, the need to coordinate public and voluntary resources is stressed. Less effort is devoted to mobilising private resources, more to producing a coordinated attack by public and voluntary agencies acting in unison. The integration of all public and voluntary agencies having impacts at the local level is a high priority.

7.34   Thirdly, the Community Developer emphasises the need for local communities to identify their own problems and to adopt their own ways of dealing with them. He thus requires that a fairly high degree of autonomy and discretionary authority be retained by local communities themselves, as represented by their local authorities (normally the district councils). Central government's relationship with local government would be focused upon achieving conformity with published and approved national policy to ensure national strategic objectives are adhered to and, especially, that local authorities have a fair share of the available stock of resources in relation to their needs.

7.35   The implication of these suggestions is clearly that the system of government would be much less hierarchical than under the corporatist model but, paradoxically, most supporters of the Community Developer's approach also call for a more coordinated attack on urban problems. The two seem difficult to combine. Neighbouring local authorities will always be to some extent in competition with one another in attracting scarce public and private resources. But with the Community Developer, competition would surely become much more overt. Rather than attempt to *avoid* overlap and replication, a more pluralistic form of government would need to be encouraged. Concurrent functions and competition between local authorities would be applauded for the contribution they make to innovation and increased efficiency, rather than criticised for their wasteful duplication, in much the same way that markets are applauded for the benefits, rather than the waste, generated by competition between firms.

The Compleat Planner

7.36   This is the last and most radical of the views of planning discussed here. Much of what was noted of the Corporatist is repeated but the Compleat Planner wants government to be given much greater direct powers over the allocation and use of society's scarce resources—whether they be labour, capital or land. The private sector would be much less important as the initiator of development. Instead of various incentives and inducements to encourage private developers to use and alter land and buildings in desirable ways, and instead of bargains being struck between government and the private sector, the 'planning authority' becomes the major initiator of development or the major developer, and exercises control and direction over all available resources including any privately owned land. Public ownership would be advanced in many sectors of the economy including a much increased public stake in land.

7.37   Town and country planning would be meshed in with other forms of planning, such as labour planning and the planning of capital, so that the emphasis is not on land related problems or goals per se. What is important is the role which land use allocations and development initiatives can play with respect to these social problems. Land development would be controlled and promoted so as to take full account of social and economic considerations, as well as the traditional and more narrowly related physical and environmental criteria.

7.38   There would be a fully planned alternative to the market: a national plan to indicate how resources would be allocated and economic activity developed, to show which sectors of the economy would be advanced and how economic activity would be distributed around the country and through time. Subordinate to the national plan would be regional plans, prepared by elected regional councils, coordinating public sector expenditure and activity within each region and providing a framework for the negotiation of 'planning agreements' between the state and private firms or statutory undertakers. Planning agreements would concentrate on economic and employment issues but would also be concerned with the social and economic need (not just market demand) for the commodities being produced and the environmental acceptability of products and production processes.

7.39   Planning would aim to produce greater equality of access—in both economic and physical terms—to employment opportunities, to needed facilities and to the final commodities produced in the economy. Thus inter-regional inequalities would be the subject of measures of positive discrimination.

7.40   National and regional plans would cover five to ten year periods of programmed public investment and private sector resource use, and would be regularly reviewed and revised according to changing needs, priorities and circumstances. Local authorities would produce, within the context provided by national and regional plans, community plans—and again these would be subject to regular review and updating. None of these plans— national, regional, community—would be restricted in their entirety to matters relating to the physical environment and land use and development, but of course these issues would be included and indeed might justify treatment in separate documents.

7.41   The kind of settlement geography advocated by the Compleat Planner would, it is supposed, depend on the outcome of democratic procedures and thus the views of a wider canvass of public opinion than is currently heeded. But typically it is suggested that a likely settlement pattern and strategy might incorporate:

Conservation of agricultural land, energy, and natural resources;

Protection of the physical environment from all forms of pollution;

Socially worthwhile production and employment activities;

An architectural style not characterised by the symbolism of corporate power;

Safe and attractive residential environments, closely integrated with places of work;

A comprehensive public transport and cycle way system;

140

Towns and regions with equal physical access to needed public facilities and employment opportunities for all residential locations.

Some of these aims would be agreed by all of our characters, most of them by one or two: the critical difference is over how they should be fulfilled and by whom. What distinguishes the Compleat Planner is his belief that they can be best and perhaps only be achieved by public authorities.

7.42 Finally, the Compleat Planner has fairly firm ideas concerning the specialist role of the planning professional. At the very least the professional should produce and make publicly available as comprehensive an assessment as possible of the likely social, economic, environmental and energy impacts of any plan or development proposal. In addition the planner would be committed to promoting social equity, protecting the environment and ensuring adequate conservation of environmental resources. The professional's main role would thus be to promote the community's self awareness, development and liberation, and to encourage a sensitivity to alternative socio-economic and physical strategies, by way of disseminating information which is free of domination by sectional interests.

PART IV CONCLUSIONS

Chapter 8 Principles: The Proper Aspirations for Planning

8.1 The bones of our position should by now be clear. We think that the planning system cannot be a neutral or technical device— its structure must reflect views on issues which are in the most general sense political and the only way to achieve organisational effectiveness is to confront and resolve political differences. We are agnostic about the market, but we do believe that where land use is concerned the market cannot be left entirely to its own devices. We think the present division of responsibilities for planning between central and local government is wrong, largely because it is based on the assumption that central government should steer the system by detailed intervention rather than by providing a general framework of policy. We regard a wide range of considerations as relevant to planning and favour a modest, diverse and flexible application of planning principles. We perceive no uniquely desirable settlement pattern, nor unique set of social and economic goals for planning to achieve. We support a promotional as well as a regulatory function for planning. Although we are in favour of the strengthening of the means of public participation in planning, and in certain circumstances of the creation of special agencies to carry out agreed policy, we think the main responsibility for planning, both plan making and development control, should remain with elected multi-purpose local authorities, with a possible role for neighbourhood and regional institutions. We believe that planners are bound to be generalists, but that where they have to serve two masters, the local planning authority and the public, they had better work individually for one or the other. We believe that planning must have a time-scale proportionate to the issues with which it has to deal, but should never pretend to certainty or commit itself to inflexible visions of the future. And finally we believe that there is a case for extending the reach of planning control to cover some if not all rural land uses.

8.2 To put these views into a coherent set we have to ask first what we expect the planning system to do and secondly what charac-

143

teristics it should exhibit. Then we shall make specific recommendations for how to get there.

The purposes of planning

8.3 *To monitor and control the impact on the environment of present and future uses of land:*
This goes beyond present responsibilities both because it extends to all kinds of land use but also because it applies to present land uses and not simply to changes of land use. Planning has a central role in evaluating whether the existing use of land and of proposed changes to land use are having, or are likely to have, a beneficial or deleterious effect on the local environment. As part of the wider political process it has a specific role in determining which public actions are likely to improve the local environment.

8.4 *To anticipate and prevent the perpetration of nuisances:*
This is a classical function of development control, not glamorous, but sensibly exercised, of great public benefit.

8.5 *To provide a coherent and consistent framework for the operation of the land market in property and development land.*

8.6 *To reconcile conflicting demands for land as they arise from the development plans of private and public agencies:*
The critical requirement here is for adequate knowledge of the intentions of developers, particularly those in the public sector, including central government departments, whose investment plans have long term implications for land use.

8.7 *To assist in the promotion of whatever developments public and private are considered desirable by the relevant public authority:*
This role, as handmaiden to responsible development, requires cooperation within local authorities, and between local authorities and other agencies of government, and with private developers.

8.8 *To provide the information necessary for the effective discharge of these functions:*
This involves not only a duty on planning authorities to collect and make available relevant information, but a system designed to provide incentives for all concerned with land use to share information about their activities and intentions on a regular basis.

What would be the characteristics of such a system?

8.9 *Comprehensiveness:*
Every body whose activities have significant implications for land use, including all public bodies, should fall within the ambit of planning control.

8.10 *Transparency:*
Every body, central or local, public or private, should be required to inform other relevant bodies of intended actions with implications for land use.

8.11 *Connectedness:*
Planning authorities should bring together this information, identify, make known and if possible resolve potential conflicts.

8.12 *Diversity:*
Central government should concentrate on the clear articulation of strategic policies of national significance and within that framework leave a large degree of discretion to local planning authorities.

8.13 *Accessibility:*
Planning authorities should give added attention to making accessible to the public the process of plan making and the handling of planning decisions.

8.14 *Modesty:*
All involved in planning should acknowledge the endemic shortage of knowledge and foresight as well as of resources and be content to live with uncertainty and change, no matter how far ahead they are obliged to look.

Chapter 9   Recommendations

9.1   Town and country planning is a means to an end, not an end itself and it is a means of securing the wider aims and objectives of our society as mediated through central and local government. Planning should not therefore be confined to issues of land use, but must be broadly defined and be coordinated with the use of other resources. What is required to make planning, thus broadly defined, effective is first a recognition of what planning can and cannot do: it is necessary to abandon not only in deed but in thought the assumptions underlying the present system of structure plans and to accept planning as a continuous process, in which aims and expectations are continually revised. Secondly we believe that for the vast majority of planning decisions the effective knowledge and the affected interests are purely local and that the planning system ought therefore to allow for a much greater degree of local choice. Thirdly we recognise that local discretion can be exercised only if national interests are not simply protected but clearly articulated: local planning must incorporate national policy and can only do so if central government makes explicit its own priorities and intentions. For this to be possible far more needs to be done to achieve internal consistency between the policies of different departments both in central and local government, and incentives have to be built into the system to increase the probability of cooperation between the tiers of governmental authority and with the other principal agents of development. Lastly we believe that much greater effort is required to make the planning system open and accountable and to encourage public involvement at the local level. We discuss each of these questions—Planning as Process, Local Discretion, National Policy, Consistency and Cooperation, and Public Accountability—in turn and make recommendations, which are summarised in Chapter 10.

Planning as process

9.2   Lip service is often paid to the notion that the very activity of planning should be seen as a process. The argument is clear enough. Plans cannot be made once and for all, set as it were in aspic. Plans are concerned with shaping the physical environment and changes in that environment take a long time. Many factors upon which the plan depends may change: new problems may emerge, new goals may be adopted and old ones discarded. Fresh opportunities and new constraints may appear so that the plan becomes inadequate, even irrelevant, as a means for reaching the original ends or for coping with unanticipated problems. In the attempt to influence our environment, our understanding of the complex relationship between ends and means continually changes. In such circumstances it is essential that planning itself should be continuous: plans must be monitored and reviewed, revised and updated to maintain the correspondence between the aims and the means of government intervention in land use and land development.

9.3　All this is commonplace and widely accepted: and yet too many examples of 'blueprint' planning remain. Intention and practice diverge. One reason is that public authorities are not obliged or even encouraged to keep to timetables when producing or approving plans. The DOE for example has had a lamentable record with the time it has taken to approve structure plans and structure plan revisions. This arises partly from a failure to concentrate on essentials: the DOE has been determined to consider every aspect of each plan rather than confine its attention to those matters which concern central government only—the relationship of structure plans to national and regional policies, their major financial and resource implications, and the need to ensure that the current statutory procedures have been followed. Insofar as the DOE regards other issues as matters of concern to central government, it should make known in advance what they are. It appears moreover that the DOE will not accept the submission of a formal alteration to a structure plan until the first submitted plan has been approved, and will not permit submission of a second alteration while the first is being processed. These administrative procedures can slow down the promulgation of plans and reduce their effectiveness in practice.

9.4　Too many planning authorities have shown themselves incapable of keeping their development plans up to date by routine and frequent monitoring, review and modification, whether these be structure, borough or local plans, and formal or informal, though structure plans present the most severe problems. They are defeated in part because the original development plans are too complicated and this in turn stems from the absence of any strict timetable for the preparation of plans, which tempts the planning authority to spend too long in collecting information and elaborating its proposals. The danger of this vicious circle is obvious. And yet some authorities have shown what can be done: East Sussex is a notable example. Most authorities when starting out to produce their development plans seem to have acted on the assumption that no planning work had ever been done before by themselves or their predecessor authorities. Other authorities realised that rather than start from scratch it would be much better to take existing policies,

148

to review and revise them regularly, and to introduce new policies as needed. The idea of policy (or planning) as a continuously modified flow is no doubt affected by the possibility of more abrupt alterations as a result of changes in the political control of a local authority. But this possibility is used as an excuse to delay commitment to plans in the short term in the hope of getting them 'right' in the long term. The only way to get local authorities where this view prevails to adopt a process style of planning (quick commitment, rapid modification), is to impose a strict timetable on their forward planning. We suggest the need to introduce a statutory cycle of three years for the review and modification of development plans, with changes permitted within the cycle if necessary, and a recognition that not everything has to be reviewed: where conditions remain unchanged a 'nil return' should be permissible. A rapid review cycle does not of course imply that the time scale of the plan itself should be short. We recognise that public participation acts as a brake on the speed with which such a cycle can be operated. But once more there are local authorities whose experience suggests that public participation can itself be strictly timetabled without any great loss of accountability.

9.5   Progress towards the acceptance of planning as an iterative continuous process has gone much further with some authorities than with others. One major disadvantage of the present uneven practice is the difficulty of synchronising the cycle of development planning with the cycles associated with investment planning or corporate planning in the public sector as a whole. Development plans are frequently out of date in relation to decisions made on public expenditure, particularly where projects involving capital expenditure are concerned. Changes in investment or financial commitments may be made which are not reflected in development plans, especially when they are made by public authorities other than those responsible for development planning. Such changes invite misunderstandings and accusations of arbitrary decision making. Their consequences are often unfortunate. This is most unsatisfactory; what is required is a much closer relationship between the cycle of physical planning and that of social and economic planning.

9.6   A further and related difficulty has been the lack of attention given when plans are formulated to the problems of putting them into practice. Though planning authorities are required to have regard to the likely availability of the resources needed to implement their proposals, the disjunction between the planning and investment cycles makes this difficult to achieve. A shorter planning cycle would enable planning authorities to take more account of the availability of resources and to modify plans accordingly. Realistic assumptions about the availability of resources, whether they be financial resources from central government, the authority's own material resources or its powers of development control, or the goodwill and cooperation of various implementing agencies (statutory undertakers and so forth), need to be fed into the planning process at an early stage and kept continually under review. Indeed a financial forecast covering several years ahead is an essential ingredient of any realistic plan.

9.7 We cannot emphasise too strongly the importance of central government's attitude to local finance. It is important to distinguish here between the level of local government expenditure, which must be a matter for political decision by central government, and the form and consistency of the methods of grant allocation. We do not wish to enter into an argument about how much central government should allow local government to spend, but whatever the level there should be some degree of continuity and stability in the policies for local authority capital borrowing and grant allocations and clearly defined powers for local government to raise revenue from the local community. Central government must exercise its undoubted discretion with restraint and also be prepared to give information about its own intentions if there is to be any sensible planning or budgeting by local authorities.[1]

9.8 Planning as a process is not a weak option: while it avoids the inflexibility and increasing irrelevance of the 'blueprint', it requires from politicians and their advisors a commitment to decide in advance on what is a desirable future and how to get there, to make decisions in accordance with this original vision and to make sure that individual policies and projects are compatible with it. It is in strict contrast to the policy of incrementalism or drift where decisions are made ad hoc to meet each problem or crisis as it arises, with no view as to the desirable direction of change or at least with no framework within which to judge decisions as they are made. But process planning should provide flexibility to ensure that the planning system, and the decisions made within it, respond to changing social and economic circumstances, changing views and priorities, and improvements in our understanding of complex physical, social and economic forces. It is *independent* of the scale of government activity, compatible with more, but also with less, government intervention than we have at present.

9.9 Planning should be flexible. The policies and programmes it produces should be capable of change, if found wanting. Each decision should be taken with awareness of the options it will foreclose for the future as well as the problems it will solve now. Land use and development require a long view, and public sector decisions now are too often made without any framework of policy or plan at all, or else with a framework which is hopelessly out of date.

Local discretion

9.10 In planning, as in other aspects of government, a balance has to be struck between the demands of the centre and the locality. We set out below (paras 9.35 to 9.42) our views on the need for a much clearer articulation of national priorities and policies: here we wish to affirm our belief that within the essential national framework local authorities should be given as much discretion as possible to control and shape their physical environment in response to the views of their local electorate. We regret that the present trend is against local discretion and variety and towards a uniformity which can be departed from only by central government initiative. An enterprise zone (EZ), a simplified planning zone (SPZ), a partnership, an urban development grant or corporation provide variety, but they have the effect of forcing local authorities to dance to Whitehall's tune, to skew their plans and proposals to meet central government criteria which may well run counter to local needs and local preferences. The fault is not all on the side of central government. Local authorities have room to innovate if they so choose. There was for instance the opportunity under earlier legislation for local authorities to set up the equivalent of an EZ or SPZ, and some did so. Local authorities have to learn to take the initiative: when they know what they want they can usually find the statutory authority to do it. But too often local authorities feel themselves obliged to bow to central government intervention in order to secure its funds.

Unwarranted centralisation
9.11 Recent trends clearly reveal an unwarranted degree of centralisation of decision making in development planning. Since 1979, for example, central government has taken a number of effective powers away from local government: in the case of urban district councils and special development orders; on enforcement actions against unauthorised small businesses (Circular 22/80); in relation to the extension of houses and industrial premises (1981 General Development Order Amendment); as a result of the abolition of the Greater London Council; in many of the Secretary of State's modifications to several structure plans prior to approval

151

and reversal of development control decisions upon appeal; and in increased controls over and new cutbacks in local government expenditure on development projects. Moves in the opposite direction have failed to compensate in any measure for this concentration of power and this process should be reversed and decentralisation of powers extended. There is little justification for central government involvement in the minutiae of the vast majority of decisions on development control and investment. There are evidently structural reasons for this centralising tendency in development planning. One is the nature of the system for the approval of structure plans: the need for every policy in every single plan to go through the approval process means that central government investigates a level of detail which is doubly inappropriate given the division of planning responsibilities between the district and county councils and the wish of the county council to stamp its authority on the local planning process in its structure plan. We say more about this below. A further reason for centralisation is the narrow role which central government has assigned to planning itself. To develop the role local authorities play as custodians of their local environments we wish to see their planning powers broadened. This could be done in a number of ways.

Local discretion over the compass of planning control
9.12   Local authorities should be given much greater powers over developments within their territories. We are aware of the difficulties associated with proposals to extend the definition of development to include such matters as the demolition of buildings or the removal of woodlands, but development control, as nationally defined, should be extended to include:

(a)   'Development' by statutory undertakers government, departments, other local authorities and other government agencies, with the exception of developments designated as being in the interests of national security by central government;[2]
(b)   Agricultural buildings and building extensions, and the construction of new farm roads.

Circular 22/80 states that aesthetic considerations are not 'material' outside environmentally sensitive areas. Our view however is that aesthetic considerations are material and are and always have been an important aspect of amenity, affecting the character of any area.

9.13   We consider that local authorities should be the sole judges of whether or not SPZs should be established in their areas. Central government should offer advice on their possible uses, form and content perhaps through a 'model' SPZ development order so that a local authority could if it wished adopt standards which were nationally recommended, bearing in mind the extra resources which might be required. The present SPZ proposals look to be another example of a centrally directed and controlled instrument rather than a means for the expression of local initiative. The SPZ document would specify which particular types of development within the zone would not require planning permission and all other changes would be subject to control, rather than grant permission automatically to all changes except those specifically excluded. To curb possible abuse, all SPZs would have to be designated in development plans.

Planning considerations

9.14   One of the most frequent criticisms of the exercise of development control by local authorities is that the decisions are made ad hoc: that local authorities expend much time and effort (and engage others in the process) in producing development plans and then proceed to ignore them, by making decisions on grounds other than those included in their plans, which may of course be out of date. It is the very existence of the 'other material considerations' component of development control, in S.29(1) of the 1971 Act, constrained by the Directive in respect of applications for developments involving departures from the development plan, which allows for this possibility. We do not wish to see the 'other material considerations' component abolished. It allows an important element of flexibility into the planning process. Nor do we wish to see imposed too rigid a definition of 'other material considerations'. But there is room for improvement: ad hoc decisions, or at least decisions not in accordance with pronounced policy should be made only with good reason. Our suggestions for emphasising planning as a process and for localising the plan making process will help to reduce the occasions when plans fail to include relevant considerations.

9.15   The general test applied in the courts that 'any consideration which relates to use and development of land is capable of being a planning consideration',[3] sensibly places the emphasis on the circumstances of each application and means that no exhaustive list of material considerations can be produced. But there are some areas where the courts and the DOE, via circulars, in being called upon to 'define by example' have erred on the side of caution, especially in their implicit definitions of what relates to the 'use' of land. Some of these we have mentioned previously. Others include

153

the financial viability of the project itself; the morality of the land use activity (for example, betting shops); and educational policy objectives. As was said in a recent House of Lords decision by Lord Scarman quoted at the beginning of this Report (and agreed unanimously by all the Law Lords sitting in that case):

'The human factor is always present, of course, indirectly as the background to the consideration of the character of land use.'[4]

We take the 'human factor' in planning to embrace all factors aimed at improving social and economic welfare. If planning is seen as involving the coordination of programmes on a spatial basis, then it must inevitably deal with social and economic developments in the context of their location.

9.16 Another problem relates to the artificial distinction made between 'planning' and 'other areas of government activity carried on by local authority or Government departments through different statutory powers'.[5] While the courts have recognised the inevitable overlaps between planning and issues relating to education facilities, pollution control, traffic considerations, housing need and so forth, the view of central government has been that it is not 'desirable that planning control should be used to secure objects for which provision is made in other legislation'.[6] It may well be that other government powers are more appropriate than those contained in the Town and Country Planning statutes but if an elected local authority acts within its planning powers broadly defined, then it should not matter that it may act similarly under alternative powers.

9.17 To the extent that a broad interpretation of planning powers may be thought likely to give rise to abuse of discretion, we feel that the double safeguard of appeals (to a tribunal—as proposed below, or to the Secretary of State as now existing) and then on a point of law to the courts, provides sufficient control against irrational, unfair or discriminatory treatment (such as the refusal of planning permission to private schools or hospitals, multinational corporations, or to restrict economic competition). In addition to the appeal to the courts there also exist the general powers of the courts to review official discretion and a history of their willingness so to do.

Infrastructure and planning gain
9.18 Although we think there could be a legitimate reason for refusing an application in the difficulty of accommodating the development because of limitations in the physical infrastructure—

154

roads, drains and sewers, water supply—we do not wish to see considerations of this kind used to stifle otherwise acceptable initiative and enterprise. We would not, for example, support refusal if it were based on the lack of publicly funded infrastructure, where private sector provision is feasible, though we recognise that there may be situations in which the provision of services by the private sector, such as retirement homes on the south coast, may in turn produce exceptional demands on public, social and medical services, which local planning authorities may want to resist. Nor would we support refusals on the grounds that development is premature if private funding were available. We understand the desire to make the most efficient use of public funded infrastructure, but if the private sector can and is likely to respond to a new development by providing the necessary infrastructure and the development is otherwise acceptable, then it should be given planning consent. And if a development is merely premature, a condition on the timing of the development should be possible in place of a refusal designed to forestall overload on the infrastructure. To do otherwise is a recipe for stagnation.

9.19   We take a similar view in respect of 'planning gain', that is contributions by the developer of land, buildings or facilities. Often the development proposal itself would generate the need for 'social infrastructure', such as schools, health, recreational or other community facilities, without which the proposal would not be acceptable. We see every merit in allowing local authorities to achieve positive benefits of this kind through their powers of development control. In this regard we have been impressed by the way in which some local authorities have obtained planning gain by organising competitions among private developers for particular sites and within broadly defined guidelines for design, density and use.

9.20   The abandonment of development land tax (DLT), announced in the budget speech on 19 March 1985, has left a gaping hole in planning policy on the whole issue of *betterment*. Now DLT has gone, there remains no means, apart from capital gains tax, whereby increases in development values which are a direct result of public sector investment can be returned to the public sector which creates them. DLT was never well integrated into the planning system and the need is now for an approach to betterment which will help the planning system to achieve its goals, such as the development of the inner city rather than the development of greenfield sites, and yet will not discourage the bringing forward of land for development. A sophisticated policy on planning gain could do just that.

155

9.21　We take a fairly wide view of what constitutes planning gain. Certain safeguards would have to be adopted. First of all 'gains' should be used for planning purposes only—that is, to improve the pattern of development and land use—and be applied to the infrastructure or environment of the community which has created the incentive, and be seen to do so. Secondly the value or benefits from the gain, in terms of planning purposes, should exceed any planning losses or costs associated with the development. Thirdly 'gains' should accord with a predetermined planning gains policy incorporated in the development plan. Finally, planning gains should never be required when the proposal without the gain achieves acceptable standards.

Greater efficiency in development control
9.22　Our discretionary planning system, and especially develop-ment control procedures, may become congested and produce unpredictable and unwarranted delays in the consideration of planning applications. This must be avoided wherever possible and we consider a number of measures to that end.

9.23　First of all we were tempted to revive proposals discussed by the Dobry Report on development control by advocating the introduction of a deemed consent procedure for all planning applications not decided upon within a specific time. We would prefer this as a method of speeding up planning decisions to streamlining development control by altering the GDO and the Use Classes Order as has been done in the past. That is far too crude a device: many small scale developments and changes do have an adverse impact on the environment. On the other hand we are not entirely convinced of the necessity. DOE figures indicate that some 90 per cent of all decisions are made within 13 weeks, and the spectacular delays of which so much complaint is made by the development industry, are not due to the planning process so much as to problems of land ownership and the failure of central government to make up its mind about policy. In any event it is probable that a deemed consent procedure would not work for planning any more than it did for building regulations: local authorities simply issued refusals. Experience in France and West Germany points in the same direction.

9.24　A second suggestion which may help to reduce delays in dealing with planning applications, is that made above to allow local authorities to develop their own versions of SPZs as and when they see fit. Since we wish to see all development coming within the compass of development control, a third proposal is to introduce a procedure through which statutory undertakers, government departments and local authorities may submit 'Development Programmes' for approval by planning authorities, still under the deemed approval regime. Such a development programme would represent an agency's projects covering a number of sites for the next three years or so. Prior arrangement between the planning authority and the agency over the timing of this kind of application would minimise disruptive effects on the planning authority's workload. Such approval of development programmes might also be integrated into the cycle of plan reviews and apply to the programme of any developer, whether from the public sector or not.

An environmental surveillance system

9.25   For planning authorities to be effective custodians of their local environment requires something more than the exercise of development control. At the moment development control constitutes a 'point of entry' control system: a decision is reached on the desirability of a development proposal at a single point in time. And yet the desirability of a development can frequently change. Provision for the revocation and modification of unused planning permissions, and more important the discontinuance of established developments, exist but because of restrictions on their use are rarely applied. The ability of the planning authority to ensure the maintenance or improvement of environmental quality is thus significantly impaired. We suggest an increase in the resources made available for the revocation and modification of unused planning permissions and the discontinuance of developments; abolition of the requirement to have revocation, modification and discontinuance orders confirmed by the Secretary of State and its replacement by a power to call in such orders when issues of national policy are raised; and though there should still be compensation for abortive work, abolition of the need to compensate for any loss in development value in the case of the revocation and modification orders, the provisions of which seem curiously out of date and inconsistent with other principles of compensation.[7] There should however continue to be a right of appeal, which should be to the planning tribunal proposed below.

9.26   Secondly, enforcement powers and procedures are cumbersome. When a breach of planning control occurs—when someone develops without planning permission or ignores conditions imposed on a permission—the law is that an enforcement notice is issued only if local authorities 'consider it expedient to do so having regard to the provisions of the Development Plan and to any other material considerations'.[8] However local authorities are advised to show that such action is adopted *'only* where planning reasons *clearly* warrant such action', where planning objections are 'insuperable',[9] and, in relation to small businesses only 'in the last resort'[10]. Enforcement action is designed both to punish and to prevent breaches of planning control. Without firm resolve it is likely that current policies will simply store up problems for the future. More and more plans will be statements of hope rather than indications of what will be done. We have received evidence that this is already happening. To counter this trend the various administrative obstacles against the use of enforcement notices should be removed, enforcement action against any breach of planning control should be required unless inexpedient, and fines for breaches should be increased, or more effective use should be made of injunctive procedures.

Positive planning

9.27   Up to this point our recommendations have been directed to increase the discretion of local authorities in the exercise of development control. But often the control or even management of initiatives coming from the private sector is not enough to secure the public interest in land use and development. That much has been accepted by all governments since the present planning system was first introduced. There can be little doubt that the implementation of development control is the backbone of the planning system. Yet there is a role too for a more positive and promotional side to planning, especially in the increasing number of places where economic circumstances are such that the impetus for development is no longer supplied by the private sector and cannot be taken for granted.

9.28   The most important promotional tools available to the planning system are firstly the various capital investments in land and buildings carried out by public agencies, including local authorities, and secondly the various grants and other financial incentives offered to private agents by the public sector. But such tools can only be effective if they are used to common purpose, if their use by one part of the public sector does not conflict to any significant extent with that in any other part.

9.29   Careful coordination (not imposition from above) of public sector aims and means is therefore required and to this we return below. Moreover, however combined, such tools can only be effective if sufficient resources are available to back up their use. In this respect, central government has been inconsistent in its policies towards capital expenditure by local government: we will return to this point also. Here however we simply point to shortcomings in the available instruments for promotion.

9.30   Although a great deal of effort has gone into urban renewal and especially the renovation and maintenance of derelict property, the main deficiency in positive planning still lies in this field. The private sector on its own has proved incapable of producing satisfactory conditions in many areas of our towns and cities: public action is called for. There are several reasons for the failure of the private sector to tackle urban renewal, including the extra costs compared to the cheaper and more profitable greenfield sites, a slowness to recognise the potential for profit, and the fact that the benefits from renewal projects do not pass in full to the developer as a reward for his efforts: there are important social returns which simply do not enter the private developer's calculations. Whatever the reason more needs to be done to ensure the maintenance of the physical quality of the built environment and to put a halt to its deterioration.

9.31   One possibility is to encourage, through legislation and the provision of resources, a greater role for local authorities as developers—buying up, renovating and then disposing of old and dilapidated properties at a profit. A willingness to accept lower profit margins than the private sector and a greater interest in conservation and the reuse of old buildings would be important factors here, and a prerequisite would be access through borrowing to sufficient financial resources to do the job properly. Local authorities should continue to act as developers in their own right and to enter into partnership agreements and joint ventures with private developers to the same ends.

9.32   In addition, we advocate further powers for local authorities to control the deliberate deterioration of land and property in the hands of private owners and to encourage their maintenance and improvement. We would like, for example, to see extended to cover unlisted buildings the idea behind the listed building repairs notice, which enables a local authority to execute necessary repairs, after due notice, and to recover costs from the owner of the building. There is already provision for both of these approaches to the renewal of housing, though the resources available are inadequate and procedures generally cumbersome. They should be made available for other kinds of buildings, such as factories and warehouses. Similar attention should be given to the general problem of derelict land to which the Royal Commission on Environmental Pollution drew attention more than ten years ago.[11]

9.33   The role of the Historic Buildings and Monuments Commission as watchdog should be extended to cover listed buildings owned by public authorities. Local authorities themselves, judge and jury in their own case, often fail conspicuously to maintain the listed buildings which they own. When public money is given to private bodies, whether for purposes of renewal or conservation, payment should be tied to results. In the countryside, for example, financial incentives should encourage positive acts of conservation or enhancement rather than reward inaction, the agreement *not* to develop. In this respect the approach adopted by the Wildlife and Countryside Act 1981 is woefully deficient. We have some sympathy for the argument that this enables private farmers to extract from the public purse funds which need not have been spent to achieve the same purpose. In any event a tight system of vetting projects should overcome this problem and our main disagreement with the Wildlife Act is not over the potential for abuse but over the negative approach, when what should be encouraged is positive conservation activity of the kind promoted by the Farming and Wildlife Advisory Group.

9.34   To encourage more local initiative in rural planning, we support the introduction of powers to enable local authorities to designate 'landscape control and management areas'. Within these areas certain changes related to agriculture, which would ordinarily be excluded from development control by the definition of 'development' and the GDO, would require approval, for example hedge removal and major agricultural land drainage works, especially where they would materially alter the productive potential of the land. These would be in addition to those changes in relation to agricultural buildings works brought within development control by our previous recommendations. In addition more power and resources should be made available for agreements and incentives for landscape conservation. Once again we stress the importance of carrots rather than sticks when it comes to encouraging people to do things that don't at present happen. Designation of the areas would be at the discretion of the local authority, subject to call-in powers with a time limit, if issues of national policy were raised.

National policy

9.35   We have emphasised the need to make room for greater local choice and control over development. At the same time we believe that central government, and by this we do not mean simply the DOE, must take on a more positive role in planning. Central government should produce and publish [concise and consistent statements of national policy where national interests are at stake in questions of land use and development. Central government should, in addition, make a firm distinction between national policy and national guidance and advice to other government agencies. Failure to make this distinction clearly has created inconsistency and confusion about what exactly constitutes its policy.

9.36 A central input to the planning process is essential. No one giving evidence to us has denied that and we ourselves accept it. Major public investments must be planned at a national level and few would dissent from the proposition that on such matters as energy installations, airport developments, transport infrastructure, major manufacturing plant and large new settlements, a national policy is a precondition for local planning and investment decisions. Moreover, decisions of this kind must be made within a framework of policy that covers the general distribution of population, economic activity and public investment in terms of inter-regional disparities in economic and employment opportunities; and the protection and conservation of scarce and vulnerable natural, social and manmade development resources, that is agricultural land, heritage buildings and landscapes, human communities, and depletable or damageable natural resources. On such matters central government must have a decisive say and the opportunity to ensure that local proposals as set out in development plans, and decisions made in the process of development control, reflect national policies. This of course depends on central government being prepared to commit itself to declared policies, which it has been notoriously reluctant to do. We note with acute concern the absence of clear, accessible and consistent policy statements on these crucial subjects. In particular there is a need for central government to be explicit about its policy on the national, spatial, distribution of its own capital expenditure.

9.37 We applaud recent improvements made by the Ministry of Agriculture, Fisheries and Food (MAFF) and the DOE in reducing the nonsense caused by contradictory policy statements on the importance of measures of rural conservation. However there remain many cases of confusion.

9.38 On conservation, central government's policies are indecisive and frequently weak. There needs to be a more absolute protection for sites of special scientific interest (SSSIs) and a requirement on all government agencies to further and not just take account of rural conservation. The public sector investment and spending programmes of the Department of Trade and Industry (DTI), Ministry of Defence (MOD) and Department of Employment (DE) are in apparent conflict with the regional policies of the DOE, as a result of their preferential treatment of particular places. Defence and transport expenditure for example has played a vital role in the economic expansion of towns along the M4 corridor. It is difficult to reconcile this with regional policy.

9.39   Difficulty arises over a range of other matters on which opinion differs as to whether a central input is either necessary or desirable: such matters include the amount of land made available for development of different kinds (housing, industry, etc), the mix between public sector and private sector development, the use of public power to steer development towards particular areas within regions, and the relationship between the proposals and plans of neighbouring authorities. It is most certainly a mistake to suppose that it is easy to separate local from national issues. Perhaps the best one can say is that when a central input is made on such matters central government should have a proper regard for local circumstances and preferences and only call in applications where there is clear evidence of failure to take account of national policy on national matters—that is declared central government policy; or where there is a need to reconcile or mediate between strongly held and conflicting convictions of neighbouring local authorities; or where plans are based on inadequate research or unrealistic prognoses. Whatever the reason central government intervention in local planning policy should take the form of negotiation rather than dictation. We return to this relationship below.

National land use policy
9.40   We have been impressed by the example from Scotland of its national planning guidelines and we recommend their use, suitably adapted, in both England and Wales. Indeed we propose that such national planning guidelines should be given the force of directives and become the primary instrument of central government's influence and that the requirement for the approval of development plans should be removed. These guidelines would have the following purposes:

(a)   to identify and to define the kinds of development which may raise national issues relevant to land use planning;

(b)   to set out the national aspects of land use which should be taken into account by local planning authorities in their development plans;

(c)   to suggest where there may be a need for interim development control policies in relation to national issues; and

(d)   to explain the criteria which form the basis for directions requiring certain planning applications to be notified to the Secretary of State.

9.41 The planning guidelines would be brief and set out in simple language. They would be subject to consultation between central and local government before adoption, rather on the lines of current informal consultations that have been followed for draft circulars. Such consultation would however become a formally established procedure so that it is not at the whim of central government[12]. The guidelines setting out the long term financial and investment framework should underpin central government's spatial and development policies. Much of what is at present contained in circulars could be put into the national planning guidelines. This would release the circular proper for the task of giving *advice* on planning matters or on questions of procedure.

9.42 More important, the national planning guidelines would help central government to present a more coherent set of policies than has hitherto been possible. Circulars currently in force have come from many different governments working at different times in very different circumstances. The guidelines would provide the vehicle to bring together and put into order this archaeology of past admonition, and also serve to bring greater consistency between the policies of the DOE and those of other government departments.

Appeals
9.43 One final issue of national policy direction concerns the criticism, to which we draw attention in Chapter 2, of the arbitrariness of decisions on development control. One important source has been the willingness of central government, through the Planning Inspectorate, to overturn on appeal the decisions of local authorities. The rate of appeals allowed has crept up over the last 15 years roughly from a fifth to a third (roughly 2,000). This amounts to a substantial interference with local authority discretion. It is also worth remark that in 1982 only 34 English planning applications were called in by the Secretary of State for his own determination after an inquiry. Local decisions should only be overturned in cases where there is a clear difference between the decision and *published* national policy, though there must remain an opportunity to appeal against improper and unreasonable decisions.

9.44 It must be recognised that inspectors themselves decide over nine out of ten appeals by 'transferred powers', that is, themselves, without recommendation to the Secretary of State. Of the approximately five per cent of decisions that are referred to the Secretary of State, in very few does the Secretary of State depart from the inspector's recommendation. (Excluding written representations on which there are no published figures, the Secretary of State overruled the inspector in one in four cases in 1984 and one in fourteen in 1985.)

9.45 In practice therefore the collegiate structure of the public inquiry whereby one person hears the case and another decides has been replaced by the decision of the person who heard the inquiry alone. While it may be of benefit that 'he who hears decides', the practice of a single decision-maker runs counter to accepted practice in other areas of public administration in respect of appeals (for example, supplementary appeals tribunals, rent tribunals, industrial tribunals etc). In these other areas the tribunal consists of a chairman assisted by two other persons often representing the interests involved. For example, industrial tribunals consist of a legally trained chairman assisted by lay representatives from each side of industry.

9.46 We think this model is one that should be introduced in respect of all appeals that are not called in or not otherwise designated as suitable for consideration by the Secretary of State. This would leave the existing public inquiry for the examination of issues of significant policy import. In these major cases present procedures should be supplemented by environmental impact statements (as recommended now by the EEC).

9.47 Tribunals would consist of a chairman drawn from the Planning Inspectorate (or, in a case involving a substantial legal element, a lawyer) plus two persons representative of both environmental and development interests drawn from a panel submitted to the appropriate regional office of the DOE by counties within the region. The management and training of, and provision of information to the tribunals should be provided by the regional offices of the DOE. The chief inspector should retain overall supervision of the system of appeals and the tribunals would come under the aegis of the Council of Tribunals. As at present, appeals could be made by way of written representations or open hearings.

9.48 We think that tribunals familiar with issues in their regions are likely to deal more expeditiously with appeals than the present peripatetic Inspectorate. There may well be variations in patterns of decisions from region to region (as there may be now as far as we know), but if this is thought likely to be a problem, the central storage and dissemination of planning information from the Department's database should be made available through the DOE's regional offices.

Securing consistency of planning policy within public agencies

9.49 Consistency over planning matters is vital, both within and between agencies in the public sector. Unfortunately the evidence suggests that this consistency is often lacking. Within local authorities the policies adopted on the quality and location of development are often at variance with policies on education, social services and transport. In central government the policies of MAFF, the DOE, the DTI, the Treasury and the Department of Transport openly conflict with one another.

9.50 It would be naive to suppose that in the large and complex organisations which make up central and local government consistency is readily achieved. But ways do need to be found to encourage greater unity of purpose and efficiency in performance. Land planning has to be complementary to other activities in local and central government. It is a tall order to expect local and central governments to behave as if they were single purposive agencies rather than collections of more or less autonomous departments. We would of course like to see planning policies and planning decisions at the local level brought into harness with policies for education, housing, transport, social services and so forth, just as we should like to see greater coordination between the various departments in central government. Development planning may make much better sense as part of a broader planning process encompassing social and economic as well as physical planning. The question is how to do it. We offer some modest suggestions.

Integration at the local authority level
9.51 The first step at the local authority level is to get a better fit between development planning and budgetary and capital expenditure cycles. Some local authorities have managed to accomplish this, but for many the time scale of the development planning process bears little relationship to the investment and expenditure cycle, especially where long periods are allowed to elapse between plan reviews. To some extent this appears to be the fault of planning departments who do not wish to see their role as strategic planners subordinated to those of other departments in the authority. On the other hand the fault may often lie with finance departments who think only in terms of the annual budget and fail to consider more extended horizons.

9.52 One conclusion is that local authority development plans should be part of a broader plan—though for practical purposes there is no reason why they should not be produced as separate documents. Again some local authorities have made progress in this direction while others are still only talking about it. We have been impressed by the model of the Scottish regional report system and recommend that it should be adapted to the circumstances of district and county councils in England and Wales. Each district council would then produce any further local plans (or local plan revisions) within the context provided by a district 'local report' and a county 'local report'. These would include: a view of the district's (county's) main problems, and their priority; a realistic view of what could be done in terms of money, men and management to tackle these problems; a synopsis of the development plan programme; and an indication of the guidelines and information which district (and county) authority requires from central government—all expressed in simple language. We suggest, once again, that the local reports should be reviewed and, where necessary, modified on at least a three-year cycle.

Integration at central government level
9.53   Here our analysis suggests that the DOE's tendency to circumscribe the compass of structure plans to a narrow land use basis are largely misplaced. We understand the Department's wish to restrict structure plans to proposals for the development and other use of land, both because structure plans are not the right vehicles for the social and economic policies of a local authority and because it is better *coordination* of development plans with other policies which is clearly required to develop a set of coherent policies, not their inclusion in a single document. We repeat what we have said above in relation to 'other material considerations' in development control, namely that it is clear that certain kinds of policy are so intimately related to physical planning that their separation seems artificial in the extreme—transport, housing and employment come readily to mind. Too rigid a demarcation can inhibit innovation in the design of appropriate policies: professionals and politicians develop commitments to particular departments and their plans and these loyalties obscure the wider view: the plan becomes an end in itself.

9.54   The DOE has attempted to resolve the problem by advocating: 'Non land use matters, for example, financial support, consultation arrangements and proposed methods of implementation should not be included as policies or proposals in structure or local plans . . . (but) . . . should be included in the explanatory memorandum or reasoned justification where they are relevant to a full understanding of a plan's policies or proposals or provide a context for them'. This advice has not been entirely successful.

9.55   Development plans have been accorded a leading role in part because there are no documents on economic and social planning which enjoy a comparable status. This is not satisfactory. The answer must be to acknowledge the importance of such other 'planning' documents and to relate their contents to the contents of development plans rather than to overload development plans themselves.

9.56   Demarcation disputes would become less intractable if the overlapping were acknowledged and made the occasion for colla- boration. What this requires is a more flexible attitude to the boundaries of government activities, whether they be concerned with development planning or employment or housing policy. One further issue regarding the relationships of departments in central government is the status accorded by other departments to the national policies on land use promulgated by the DOE. We have already referred to the mismatch between the spatial implications of expenditure channelled through the MOD and the regional policy supported by the DTI and DOE. Other examples include conflicts between MAFF and the DOE over the relative claims of agricultural production and conservation, and between the DE and the DOE over the spatial consequences of assistance to industry, training and employment.

9.57   There ought to be some means by which national land use and spatial policies adopted by the DOE and published, for instance, in the national planning guidelines, should inform and constrain the policies of those other departments whose decisions have con- sequences for the distribution of social and economic activity. This would of course require consultation and negotiation: as regards our own recommendation on national planning guidelines, we suggest that a procedure for review, consultation and revision, involving all relevant departments, be carried through at least once in every three years. We should point out here the importance of our earlier recommendation that all 'developments' proposed by government departments be brought within the compass of develop- ment control, which provides those departments with an incentive to cooperate.

Securing consistency between public agencies

9.58   We have stressed the importance of local discretion and the value of an emphasis on planning from the bottom up. But the choice is not between a local or a national or even a regional planning system. There have to be elements of all three. It is equally a mistake, as we have already suggested, to suppose that it is easy to divide local from regional and regional from national issues. The divisions adopted must depend on political choice and on social and economic circumstances as well as on technical considerations. What is needed is a system which permits and encourages continuing negotiation of the boundaries between national and local as changes become relevant and necessary. We have to ask ourselves what kind of system can best cope with change and with uncertainty.

9.59 As a general principle, we believe that central government should confine its attention to matters which are clearly of vital national concern, namely:

(a) The implementation of clearly stated and published national policies, including policy on the efficient use of financial resources, and especially the government's own finances, in shaping the pattern of development; and the government's priorities for expenditure between one area and another; and

(b) The resolution of conflicts and disputes between local authorities.

Judged by these criteria, it is clear that central government has adopted too embracing a view of the 'national' interest and has interfered too much in local authority affairs. Central government should only get involved in local disputes as a last resort.

The importance of local government finance
9.60 Whatever the level of local government expenditure—and this must be determined by political principles—the present system of grant finance and capital borrowing by local government is seriously flawed. Neither central government nor local government has had faith in its fairness or its permanence but if our proposals to provide greater integration between central government allocation of resources and that of local government, and to fuse resource planning with physical planning, are to have any chance of success, then a rather more stable system of local government finance is a critical and necessary condition.

The machinery of cooperation
9.61 Any proposals directed to achieving a different balance of power in planning between central and local government must provide answers to some difficult questions: how to get central government to declare its hand, how to deal with the separation of responsibility for the making and the implementation of plans, and how to resolve potential conflicts between planning authorities at the regional level. We have considered these matters at length and

have become increasingly conscious of the twin temptations which beset would be reformers. The first of these may be described as constitution-building: the temptation to tear up the organisation chart and to produce a brand new structure of institutions at central, regional and local level. We have already expressed our sympathy with the view that the present structure of government below national level is ill suited to planning and indeed that the division of functions and the coordination of policy within central government leaves much to be desired. We are equally aware that most schemes for reorganisation, however well conceived and carefully devised, have not been implemented and those schemes that have been implemented have caused enormous disruption, confusion and expense without fulfilling the expectations of their progenitors. We have therefore confined our recommendations to what can be done within the present structure of central and local government.

9.62   The second temptation is to recommend elaborate procedures to ensure the harmonious integration of planning activities within and between the various tiers of government. The danger here is to underestimate the time and cost which these admirable practices of cooperation, coordination and consultation will in fact impose: the reform of planning is a long history of the erroneous choice of timetables, because what was intended to be quick and simple proved slow and complex. Our aim has been therefore to simplify procedures and, where possible, to eliminate requirements such as the approval of development plans, which have proved so cumbersome as to defeat their own purposes.

9.63   We recognise that the twin pillars of the planning system are, and should remain, the implementation of central government policy and the maintenance by each local community of effective control over its own environment. These considerations are bound to come into conflict from time to time, and any new system must contain the means of resolving such conflict. We further recognise that, in a country with such a strong tradition of governmental centralisation, the planning system should ensure that the elected government of the day can in practice implement its chosen policies, even where they conflict with local priorities, subject only to review in the courts.

9.64   Our recommendation is that the planning system should be simplified and streamlined, by concentrating all development planning and development control powers at local level, though subject to overriding government direction. For planning purposes the metropolitan boroughs which do not now fall under the jurisdiction of any county and would for the most part prove too powerful to be subordinated to their neighbouring counties, should themselves be treated as counties, combining the functions of county and district. This is an anomaly which we cannot avoid without rectifying the anomalies of the local government structure itself. County development plans would not require approval by central government, and local plans would have to be integrated with development plans. The right of appeal to central government would be abolished (though the call-in power would be retained and developed), and the jurisdiction transferred to the planning tribunals proposed above (para 9.46 and 9.47).

9.65   As we have already discussed above (para 9.40), central government would have a new power to issue 'planning guidelines' which would in effect be binding directives, following effective consultation with local authorities and relevant public agencies. We do not propose any statutory timetable for that consultation, recognising that it should remain as at present a matter for ministerial judgement from case to case. Following promulgation, however, all planning authorities would be under a statutory duty to give effect to those guidelines in exercising both their plan making and development control functions.

9.66   We recognise that such guidelines would relate both to 'national' issues as conventionally conceived and to 'regional' issues, where coordination is required only within a regional frame. There are important matters that frequently require coordination at regional level, but we are doubtful about the case for a regional tier of government as such and have already indicated our decision to work within the existing structure of local government. The institutions of central government are the only available instruments of regional government, and are likely to remain so: this is clearly evident in Scotland, Wales and Northern Ireland, but is also substantially true of the English regions and their regional offices. The planning staff at regional office level would need to be strengthened, to handle this new regional planning function, implemented through the planning guideline system; but that development would be in line with current practice and should present no real difficulty.

9.67   This new system would recognise, we believe, the growing demand at local level for more effective, democratic control of the local environment. It is consistent with our view that the planning process should be conceived 'from the bottom up': this would represent a significant change from the present system, which still embodies the 'top-down' assumptions of the immediate post war period. Yet it would not diminish the effectiveness of central intervention where the government considered that issues of overriding national or regional policy were involved. The government would have the discretion to issue directive planning guidelines at any time, coupled with the power to call in any particular planning application at district council level. We recognise that this call in power would and should be unrestricted, but hope that it will be exercised with restraint and its use confined to issues where national or regional considerations demand it.

9.68 Our recommended system represents, we believe, a proper balance between the institutions of central and local government: it has neither a 'centralist' nor a 'localist' bias, in conventional terms. We recognise that, by creating a clear hierarchical relationship in planning matters between county and district, we are touching upon matters of constitutional and political significance which are currently under review in other respects; our concern, however, has been specifically with the planning system, where 'supra-district' coordination is of great importance, both at county and at regional level. We are satisfied that, in planning terms, it would be a mistake to move to a district only system, consisting of over 400 separate local planning authorities and a single central government; and whereas we recognise that county boundaries would in many cases benefit from substantial revision, we do not advocate the removal of a county-wide planning jurisdiction; indeed, we think it should be strengthened.

9.69 The new system would have a number of important advantages. It would simplify the machinery of central government by eliminating the requirement to approve structure plans at DOE level; this would be offset in part by the development of a stronger planning establishment at regional office level, but there would be an overall gain. By removing the requirement for approval, local plan making would become much more flexible and responsive: county councils could with greater ease ensure that their plans were up to date, and that they reflected current policy assumptions; that greater immediacy and relevance would also inform district plans. There would perforce accrue to county development plans (provided they were up to date) an authority and relevance which structure plans currently lack, and this would meet the many complaints made about their time wasting nature under present arrangements.

9.70 The change would also mean that the plan making process would be better integrated with the exercise of development control at local level. Appeals against a district council refusal of planning permission would be heard by a tribunal with nomination from the authority that had been responsible also for making the relevant plan. We believe that this integration would greatly enhance the effectiveness of local planning and strengthen local confidence in the planning process generally. Finally, in the new system, central government would never be put in the position of overturning a local planning decision: the matter would either be called in, for a single decision without appeal, or left at the district level for decision, subject only to appeal to the tribunal. This would have the political advantage of removing a major source of dissatisfaction, widely expressed by local planning authorities, with the scale of direct 'government intervention' in local matters through the centralised planning appeal system.

9.71 We recognise that these proposals place great weight on the two proposed instruments of government control, namely the 'planning guideline' directive and the calling-in jurisdiction; and it is right that we should be more specific in our recommendations in these two respects.

9.72 Our thinking about planning guidelines has been influenced by the evidence of the Scottish model, but we have not been limited to that. There are other reasons for concern about the ineffectiveness of the present system, and we have already indicated many areas in which policy guidance is widely considered to be inadequate. Our hope is that, by giving to central government the power to initiate and promulgate such binding guidelines (without waiting for the submission of structure plans), the new system will encourage the formulation of authoritative guidelines in sectors in which they are missing; they could also be used more extensively for inter-departmental coordination. Our view is, nevertheless, that all such guidelines should be issued by the DOE, and under the authority of the Secretary of State for the Environment: without that coordinating influence, the new system could generate even greater confusion and governmental dislocation. We are also attracted by the suggestion (which received wide support in the evidence submitted to us) that the DOE should publish an annual White Paper on land and the environment, on similar lines to the annual White Paper on transportation, and the government's Annual Economic Statement; such a White Paper would provide invaluable guidance to both county and district councils, in the preparation of their plans, and in the continuing process of their revision.

9.73 Binding 'planning guidelines' would be a new element in the national planning system. The second element, however, would not be new: the 'calling-in' power has been an integral element in the system since its inception in 1947. However, with an appeal system in place, the power has been little used: the operation of the appeal system has given central government all the necessary opportunities to manage the system. With the removal of centralised appeals, the calling-in procedure will for the first time operate as it was designed to operate, avoiding conflicts between different tiers of government and focusing on those matters which are considered to merit central government intervention.

9.74   We suggest that, given new and more effective notification procedures, the calling-in provisions of the legislation offer the most appropriate machinery for case-by-case intervention. In many authorities, computer-based planning records are now commonplace, and the development of a regional notification system would not present any undue organisational problems; in many sectors, central government could limit the scope of applications requiring notification. We recommend also that any party to a planning application, including neighbours and others affected, should be entitled to apply for the application to be called-in; this would merely consolidate present informal practice. We recognise that regional office staffing would need to be strengthened in order to ensure the expeditious exercise of this jurisdiction, and that this would partially offset staff savings in London; we nevertheless judge the overall solution to be right.

9.75   In formulating these proposals, we have consciously avoided going into detail on a number of important incidental matters. This is not because we have ignored them, but because we believe that the new system should allow for the emergence of a wide diversity of local and regional practice, and we would not wish to constrain that. Such matters are: the scope and content of the county development plan, and the ways in which it is integrated with district plans; the processes of public consultation both in plan making and in development control (though we do have other proposals in that regard, below); the handling of planning appeals from district level to the regional level; the organisation of the regional office function, and the formulation of planning guidelines relating to regional issues; the award of planning appeal costs; and there are others. We recognise that on many of these matters there would be important decisions to be made, which might indeed not even be regarded as 'incidental' by all those concerned. We have declined to make recommendations on these matters, so as to concentrate on the broad features of the reforms we propose.

9.76   Although we do not propose to pursue the matter in detail, it is implicit in the system which we are proposing that structure plans in their current form should be phased out and the county development plan should resemble the county report recommended by the Planning Advisory Group.

9.77   This may seem a surprising and radical proposal. But structure plans as we have seen have become of doubtful value, and it does not seem likely that modification would improve matters sufficiently to overcome the inertia which has built up in the system. Structure plans in general have not proved to be the 'process' planning documents they were originally intended to be: even those that have been revised recently have often been based on the very different social and economic conditions prevailing before 1980 and are as a result out of date.

9.78   There has been too much concentration on detail and not enough regard for the value of keeping to a timetable. Nor have structure plans proved to be an adequate vehicle for the kind of strategic planning, the need for which we have been discussing in the latter sections of this chapter. Structure plans do involve a strategic planning of sorts: they handle for instance the relationships between the different districts within the county. But there are as many strategic issues between districts of different counties as there are between districts within counties, and there is little incentive in the present system to see that these are taken into account by structure planning authorities. The resolution of regional problems is left to central government through its review of structure plan proposals. Since structure plans are often separately reviewed and at different times, it is hardly surprising if regional problems slip through the interstices of the system without adequate examination or resolution.

9.79   The evidence submitted to us permits little doubt that the main operational level in planning has become the district council, both in the rural shires and the metropolitan conurbations. District councils have inevitably tried to resist the efforts of the counties to impose their will and county structure plans have too often tried in turn to preempt district council's own plans over issues which should have been of little concern to a strategic authority. And since county councils have had little influence on the exercise of development control the detail of structure plans has been redundant. District councils have found it easy to ignore them as a serious restraint. The most frequent comment made to us about structure plans is that they have been a waste of time, money and effort.

Public accountability of the planning system

9.80 Any reversal of present trends to allow local government greater opportunities for initiative, experiment and decision in planning matters must entail an equal commitment to greater local accountability. For it has to be said that at present the accountability of local government is at best indifferent. The fact that local authorities are elected is not enough. Members of the public must have access to councillors and officers, to meetings and to papers, and opportunities to contribute to the formation of policy at an early stage. Some local authorities have already made significant progress and we hope that the Local Government (Access to Information) Act 1986 will provide the stimulus for the rest to follow suit. It is likewise important that local authorities should respond positively to complaints and to findings of maladministration by the Commission for Local Administration. Strictly these matters are outside our brief, but they are a necessary background to any proposals to maintain or enhance the role of local authorities in planning. Local government has no constitutional protection and the events of the last few years have demonstrated how weak is its political support. Greater public participation in planning is a good in itself but it would also be a means to strengthen public commitment to local government as such.

9.81 A couple of examples from existing practice may suffice to show the sort of thing we have in mind. The encouragement of public participation by the Warwick District Council in the making of local plans,[13] could be imitated by other local authorities. There, councillors were intimately involved in the preparation of a plan and the public had the opportunity through working groups and an informal public hearing to contribute to the plan in its formative stages. Other examples of community involvement in the making of local plans should also be given wide publicity by local authority associations as a counterblast to DOE circulars decrying public participation. Where planning decisions are concerned, we may draw attention to the exemplary arrangements of the Calderdale Metropolitan Borough Council for public access to the meetings of its planning subcommittee. Planning applications are advertised in a weekly list. The planning subcommittee is open to the public and meets in the early evening when many people who are at work during the day can attend. As members of the public arrive the committee clerk makes a note of the planning applications which concern them. The application which concerns the largest number of people attending is then dealt with first; that with the second largest number of interested people present next, and so on. After the planning officer has presented his assessment and recommendation on each application he is questioned in public by members of the subcommittee. A representative of any objectors present is then invited to speak and may be questioned by the subcommittee. Finally the applicant is allowed to speak and again may be questioned. The subcommittee then debates the application and reaches its decision in open session. This practice shows both a self confidence and a confidence in the public which are in themselves admirable and likely to improve the quality and acceptability of planning decisions. The many local authorities which still exclude the public from planning subcommittees altogether should take note.

9.82   Local authorities should also consider carefully the possible ways in which they may bring planning applications more effectively to the attention of the public and how the services of planners may be made directly available to the public. Again this is largely a matter of the dissemination of good practice: the ideas are widely canvassed and understood. They need to be as widely adopted.

9.83   We think the time has come to allow neighbours, amenity groups or other 'aggrieved' persons the right to appeal against the *grant* of a planning permission by the local authority to itself. Without such an appeal there is no possibility of checking the discretion of a local authority, acting in such a case as judge in its own cause, other than through the courts. This involves an expensive and lengthy process which allows review on points of law alone, and not on policy or planning judgement.

9.84   Another recent innovation is the community urban development assistance team, whose function is to assist residents in inner cities to redevelop and improve their own areas. Here community involvement is taking on a 'Third World' flavour where the community is not just talking about what it would like but is actually building it with professional assistance. This form of community involvement in planning is part of a movement, more developed in some authorities than others, to decentralise services, base them on neighbourhood units and to involve councillors and the local community in their management and delivery. This too is a development which if carefully planned and monitored could contribute to a closer link between people and local government. In this connection the case for urban parish councils, or elected neighbourhood councils, which was put to the Redcliffe-Maud Commission and enjoyed some support in the early and mid seventies, could usefully be resurrected. What is required is permissive legislation to provide a power to create such councils,

176

leaving it to individual district authorities to decide, subject to *guidance* from the centre, whether to establish such councils, and what specific functions to confer on them.

9.85   Local accountability cannot be too strongly urged. At a time when central government is, in a sense, withdrawing from people, becoming more secretive and less open to persuasion, it is of importance that local government demonstrates openness, accountability and fairness. The planning system has a crucial role to play in this matter; over the last 15 years it has on balance been in the forefront of moves towards greater participation and openness in local government.

9.86   What is needed now is a deliberate and concerted effort on the part of the local authority associations, professional organisations, and outside bodies to encourage the continuation and expansion of participation in the planning system as a spearhead of greater local accountability.

9.87   We have set out the main features of the system that we recommend in the accompanying diagram and summary.

Notes:

1   For a similar argument see the Report of the Audit Commission: 'Capital Expenditure Controls in Local Government in England', April 1985, HMSO, and in the context of university finance the Report of the Steering Committee for Efficiency Studies in Universities (2 vols), chaired by Sir Alec Jarrett, March 1985, published by the Committee.
2   In other words we would like to see the present informal procedures contained in Circulars 7/77 and 2/81 given statutory force.
3   In Stringer v Minister of Local Government and Housing (1971) 1 AER 65 at 77
4   [1984] 3 ALL E.R. p 744
5   Grant, Malcolm *Urban Planning Law* (Sweet & Maxwell 1982) p 285
6   *Development Control Policy Notes* 1
7   A further possibility here would be to reintroduce one of the Uthwatt Committee's proposals to enable local authorities to place a 'life' on non-conforming uses, at the expiry of which the use would be brought to an end without compensation.
8   Circular 22/80 para 15
9   Circular 22/80 para 15
10   Circular 22/80 Annex—para 1
11   Fourth Report of the Royal Commission on Environmental Pollution. Pollution Control: Progress and Problems. Paras 76–85. HMSO 1974. Cmnd No.5780.

12　In which connection we remark with regret the failure to circulate in draft the expected circular on planning controls over small firms.

13　Described in a DOE sponsored study 'Public Participation in Local Planning. Publicity and Communication: a case study of Warwick District Council' by M J Bruton and A J Lightbody. From the Department of the Environment.

Summary: The Proposed Planning System

Timetable

Central government

1. White Paper on land and the environment issued *annually* by Department of the Environment (DOE) after consultation with other central government departments with major investment programmes or interests in land use.
2. National planning guidelines issued by DOE as required, but all extant guidelines to be reviewed, brought up to date and made compatible with each other on a triennial cycle.
3. Call-in of planning applications involving questions of national or regional policy as required. Call-in may lead to reference to 'national' public inquiry.

Region

1. Regional version of national planning guidelines issued by DOE regional offices as required and amended following DOE triennial review.
2. Regional review incorporating national planning guidelines and proposals of central government departments, statutory undertakers, major developers and county councils issued by DOE regional office after consultation and public hearings. Reviewed and reissued on triennial cycle.

Local government

1. County strategy setting out policies, investment programmes and proposals and resource implications within lines of national planning guidelines and regional report. Reviewed and reissued triennially after consultation with district authorities.
2. County development plan incorporating land use proposals of county strategy in greater detail. Reviewed and reissued triennially after public hearings. Does not require DOE approval.
3. District and local plans drawn up in conformity with county development plan. Reviewed and reissued triennially and

submitted to county for approval.
4. Planning applications considered in light of current development plans and national planning guidelines, monitored by DOE regional office and subject to call-in by DOE or appeal to planning tribunal.

Diagram: The Proposed Planning System

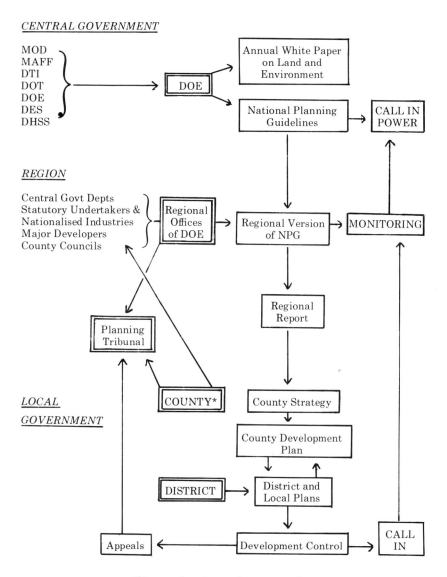

CENTRAL GOVERNMENT

MOD
MAFF
DTI
DOT
DOE
DES
DHSS
} → DOE → Annual White Paper on Land and Environment

DOE → National Planning Guidelines → CALL IN POWER

REGION

Central Govt Depts
Statutory Undertakers &
Nationalised Industries
Major Developers
County Councils
} → Regional Offices of DOE → Regional Version of NPG → MONITORING

Regional Report

Planning Tribunal

LOCAL GOVERNMENT

COUNTY* County Strategy

County Development Plan

DISTRICT → District and Local Plans

Appeals ← Development Control → CALL IN

*Metropolitan boroughs are counties

181

Chapter 10   Summary of Recommendations

1. *Central government should publish from time to time concise and consistent statements of national policy wherever national interests in land use and development are at stake, and this should be its primary planning function.*

(i)   Central government should provide clear policy statements on such matters as the need for and location of energy installations, airport developments, national transport infrastructure, major manufacturing plants and large or extended new settlements. Such statements should be made within a clear policy framework which covers:

(a)   the spatial distribution of population and economic activity;

(b)   the scale and location of scarce and vulnerable natural, social and manmade resources; and

(c)   the spatial distribution of central government's own investment programme and policies.

It is not necessary that central government should take a view on all matters affecting land use, but where it has an interest or objective it should state clearly what it is. This should be done through the medium of an annual White Paper on land and the environment (paras 9.35 to 9.39)

(ii)   Central government should introduce national planning guidelines for England and Wales, modelled on the Scottish system of national planning guidelines, and prepared on a regional basis. These would provide the medium for the policy statements recommended above and would have the following purposes:

(a) to identify and define the kinds of development and locations which may raise national issues relevant to land use planning;

(b)   to set out the national aspects of land use which should be taken into account by local planning authorities in their development plans;

(c)   to provide early warning of national developments which may require interim policies of development control; and

(d) to explain the criteria which form the basis for directions requiring certain planning applications to be notified to the Secretary of State.

The guidelines would be brief and set out in simple language. They would go through a consultative procedure with local government before adoption and be prepared on a regional basis. Much of what is currently in circulars could be put in the guidelines, releasing the circular proper for the task of giving advice on planning matters or matters of procedure (paras 9.40 to 9.42).

(iii) All planning authorities would be under a statutory duty to give effect to national planning guidelines in the exercise of their powers for plan making and development control. These guidelines would concern both national and regional issues and the regional offices of the DOE should be strengthened to handle the regional application of national policy and the resolution of intraregional problems. All such guidelines should be issued by the DOE as the coordinating department for national policy on land use and the DOE should also publish an annual White Paper on land and the environment on similar lines to the annual White Paper on transportation and the government's Annual Economic Statement (paras 9.65 and 9.72).

The call-in power should be used by central government on matters which affect national policy or where disputes between local authorities require to be resolved and this should be achieved through more effective notification procedures by regional offices of the DOE (paras 9.73 and 9.74).

This procedure would entail the phasing out of structure plans (paras 9.76 to 9.79).

(iv) Local planning authority decisions should only be over-turned on appeal where there is a clear difference between the decision and published national guidelines, or where the local authority's discretion has been exercised improperly or unreasonably (para 9.43).

2. *There should be a greater degree of consistency between land use planning and other resource planning within local authorities and central government.*

(i) There is a need for a closer integration of development planning with the budgetary and capital expenditure cycles. Development plans should be part of a broader style plan. Each district and county council should produce its development plans within the context provided by a district or a county 'local strategy', modelled on the Scottish regional report. These local strategies would include: a view of the district or county's main problems and their priority; a realistic view of what can be done in terms of money, manpower and management to tackle these problems; a synopsis of the development plan programme, and an indication of the guidelines and information which the district (and county) authority requires from central government—all expressed in simple language. The local strategies should be reviewed and, where necessary, modified on at least a three year cycle, linked with that for development planning (para 9.52).

(ii)   All parts of central government should be obliged to follow published national land use and development policies and the development plans of individual local planning authorities by applying for planning permission for any developments they wish to carry out. A review, consultation and revision procedure, involving all central government departments should be carried out at least every three years on these national planning guidelines (paras 9.57 and 9.72).

3. *There should be much greater consistency in land use and development planning between local and central government agencies.*

(i)   Central government should only get involved in disputes between local planning authorities where clear national or regional policy is at stake (para 9.59).

(ii)   The system of local government finance is in disarray. What is required is a system which minimises the uncertainties of the annual grant allocation and leaves local councils in no doubt as to their powers to raise revenue from their locality. The government has recognised that the current system of finance is unstable and does not serve government objectives or local government needs. We make no comment as to whether the level of grants, and of local government expenditure more generally, is too high. However our recommendations for greater consistency between national and local planning and for fusing physical planning with wider resource allocation decisions will be set at nought if national and local government cannot develop a more stable and constructive financial relationship (paras 9.7 and 9.60).

(iii)   In order to achieve a proper balance between central and local government in the planning process, the system should be simplified and streamlined by concentrating all development planning and development control powers at local level, subject to central government direction on national policy. County plans would not require approval by central government and local plans would have to be integrated with them as at present. The right of appeal to central government would be abolished and the jurisdiction transferred to regional planning tribunals appointed by the DOE from the Planning Inspectorate and persons nominated by the counties. The Planning Inspectorate should be reconstituted and its services be made available to assist in the management of the appellate jurisdiction (para 9.64).

4. *Local authorities should have greater choice over the definition of acceptable development and the considerations relevant to planning decisions, and should have power to make such planning decisions as affect their areas only.*

(i)   There should be much less emphasis on uniformity in the planning system and especially on a uniformity which can only be modified on the initiative of central government. Recent suggestions for modification of the definition of development to include such matters as the demolition of buildings or the removal of woodlands raise formidable practical difficulties and cannot be recommended without further investigation. Local planning control should however be extended to include changes proposed by statutory undertakers, government departments and agencies, and local authorities, and to cover agricultural buildings and building extensions and the construction of new farm roads. Local authorities should also have powers to exclude changes from planning control, including the power to designate their own simplified planning zones, in which particular types of development which did not need planning permission would be specified, leaving all other changes subject to control. Such simplified planning zones would need to be included as part of a development plan (paras 9.12 and 9.13).

(ii)   No attempt should be made to impose further limits on the grounds on which local authorities at present make their decisions on development control. The interpretation of 'other material considerations' is sufficiently wide to allow

186

other factors, besides amenity, public health and physical convenience, to be taken into account, and appeal for review by the courts is adequate to prevent abuse of local authority discretion. Aesthetic considerations should continue to be accepted as material (para 9.12).

The Department of the Environment should relax its attempts to circumscribe the compass of development plans to a narrow land use basis. Social and economic factors must be taken into account in order to include what Lord Scarman has called 'the human factor' in structure and local plans (para 9.15).

Planning control should not be limited to securing objectives for which no provision is made in other legislation, such as that concerning pollution, traffic, housing or education (para 9.16).

(iii) Development control should not be used merely to *limit* competition between land uses and land users. Nor should it be used to discriminate against particular types of developer or user, such as a multi-national firm, private school or hospital, trade union or political party, save that it would be legitimate to discriminate in favour of a local user or developer where no national interest is affected. While it would be legitimate to refuse a planning application because of pressure on infrastructure (roads, drains, sewers, schools and so forth), this reason should not be used to refuse an application which is premature or where the necessary infrastructure can and will be supplied by the private sector para 9.18).

(iv) A system should be established to improve the monitoring of applications which involve departures from approved development plans. Only those planning applications which involve matters of more than local importance should be called-in (para 9.74).

(v) The role of *local authorities* as guardians of the local environment should be strengthened. They should devote more resources to revoking and modifying unused planning permissions and to the discontinuance of developments. Revocation, modification and discontinuance orders should no longer require to be confirmed by the Secretary of State, though the power to call-in such orders should remain where issues of national policy are raised. Enforcement action for any breach of planning control must be taken more seriously, there must be strong grounds for desisting from enforcement, and fines for breaches should be increased or a more liberal use be made of injunctive proceedings (paras 9.25 and 9.26).

(vi) Control of initiatives from private developers in the public interest is not enough. Positive action is required from local authorities to implement development plans. Such action should be taken in concert with the use of control powers and in concert with the actions of other public authorities. Local authorities should take a greater role as developers: buying up, renovating and disposing of old and dilapidated property, as well as continuing to act as developers in their own right and entering into partnership agreements and joint ventures with private developers (para 9.31).

They should also have the power after due notice to execute necessary repairs on old and dilapidated buildings and to recover the costs from the owner. Attention should also be given to the reclamation of derelict land (para 9.32).

(vii) The Secretary of State should consider an extension of the powers of the Historic Buildings and Monuments Commission to cover listed buildings owned by public authorities (para 9.33).

(viii) Local authorities should be permitted and encouraged to follow current practices as regards planning gain in positive experiments, subject to the adoption of a definite policy to be included in their development plans, and the proviso that planning gains should never be required when the proposal without the gain achieves acceptable standards (para 9.21).

(ix) Public grants to private developers should be tied to results: financial incentives should encourage positive acts, whether of conservation or improvement, rather than reward agreement not to develop (para 9.33).

(x) Local authorities should be empowered to designate 'landscape control and management areas', where certain designated changes, such as hedge removal or major drainage works on agricultural land, would require approval, and additional powers and resources would be made available or agreements and incentives to conserve and enhance the landscape. If issues of national policy were raised, such plans would need to be lodged with the county and within a time limit would be subject to call-in (para 9.34).

5. *The planning system should be made more accessible and accountable to the public.*

   (i)   Councillors should be more closely involved in the preparation of plans and the public should be given the opportunity to contribute to the formation of plans in their early stages and not only of consultation after the main lines of the plan have been decided. The local authority associations should give wide publicity to good examples of community involvement in the making of local plans. Equal attention should be given to examples of good practice in the hearing of planning applications (paras 9.80 and 9.81).

   (ii)   Local authorities should consider more effective means for bringing to the attention of the public all planning applications (para 9.82).

  (iii)   There should be a right of appeal for neighbours or other 'aggrieved' persons against the grant of a planning permission by a local authority to itself (para 9.83).

  (iv)   All local authorities should adopt the practice of making directly available to the public the services of professional planners (para 9.84).

6. *Throughout the system, planning should be a continuous process, not the production of a blueprint. It should involve regular monitoring and frequent review and modification of plans, and have regard to the efficiency and costs of the planning process.*

   (i)   *Central government* should confine its attention to those aspects of plans which affect declared national and regional policies or have major implications for the provision of finance or other resources (para 9.3).

   (ii)   *Local authorities* should be obliged to follow a three year cycle for the review and modification of their development plans. They should not start to plan from scratch at the beginning of each cycle, but revise adapt and modify existing policies as necessary. They should attempt to synchronise the cycle for land use and development planning with their cycles for financial, social and economic planning. When preparing plans they should pay more attention to the availability of the resources necessary to implement them, whether these be land, manpower, finance or political authority. They should pay particular attention to the resources available to the other agencies in both public and private sectors which will have to implement the plans in practice. Given the time money and effort which will be expended in producing plans and keeping them up to date, central and local government should both be firmly committed to the plans and resist major departures from them on ad hoc grounds. In the exercise of development control decisions should be taken with due regard as to whether or not they will close down future options as well as meet current needs (paras 9.4 to 9.6).

Appendix I   The Original Brief

1. Terms of reference

To inquire into the assumptions and purposes of the town and country planning system, its past and present performance and its proper role in the future; and to report.

In interpreting these terms of reference particular attention will be paid to:

(a) The philosophy rather than the mechanics of planning;
(b) Comparison with the experience of planning overseas;
(c) The growing relevance of the law and practices of the European Community to planning in Britain.

2. Questions to be addressed

The system of town and country planning has evolved from an initial concern with physical aspects of urban design, through social policy (garden cities, new towns), to economic policy (regional policies, job creation), and major issues of national policy (energy policy, conservation). The operation of the system has also changed in significant ways since the Town and Country Planning Act of 1947. This evolution has to be kept in mind in assessing what was expected of the system in the past, what should be expected in the future, and given agreement on the scope and purposes of planning what institutional arrangements are appropriate and necessary. The Inquiry will therefore consider:

(a) *Evolution and performance*

   (i) What if any were the underlying assumptions, purposes and goals of the system of planning set up under the sequence of Town and Country Planning Acts?

  (ii) How were these expressed in legislative and administrative terms?

 (iii) What have been the significant changes in the operation of the system since its inception?

 (iv) How successful has the developing system been in accomplishing its aims in practice?

  (v) How far have its aims and achievements given satisfaction to those responsible for their invention and implementation and to those who have had to live with the results; that is to politicians and officials, national and local, planners and other professionals, directly affected interests and other less directly affected publics?

 (vi) How have the outcomes of the system compared with those in other countries? In what respects have we done better or worse?

(vii) Insofar as there has been dissatisfaction has this arisen because of disagreement about the aims, because of failure to achieve the aims adequately, for want of the necessary powers and resources, or because of disenchantment with the original aims once achieved?

(viii) If there is disenchantment, has this arisen from disappointment with the intended results, concern about the unforeseen by-products of the planning process, changes in society itself, or the failure of the system to adapt to new problems or priorities?

(ix) If the system has failed to adapt to new problems and priorities, what are they and might they form a new basis for the planning system?

(x) If so, what changes in the system would be necessary?

(b) *Expectations and aspirations*

(i) Scope

Which of the following should the planning system attempt to encompass, whether in the private or the public interest, or for the resolution of conflicts between private interests and between private and public interests:

—The control of nuisances or disbenefits arising from development;

—The extraction of an element of public benefit by bargaining over development;

—The control over development as part of a positive notion of the wider public interest, the encouragement of 'appropriate development' and the attempt to redistribute social benefits;

—The attempt to coordinate the control and development of land use with the allocation of other resources, locally or nationally.

(ii) Timescale

What are the implications of different scopes or levels of planning for the timescale of planning? Are the different timescales compatible with one another: do low level small decisions preempt high level large ones? How can uncertainty about long term trends be reconciled with the necessity to make decisions with long run implications for land use?

(iii) Information

What would an ambitious scope for planning require in the way of up-to-date knowledge of changes in environmental land use and other relevant economic and social data; and what in the way of assessments, forecasts, projections or scenarios? What are the technical problems and what are the costs of providing such information? What institutional arrangements are necessary, especially with a view to obtaining alternative judgements and proposals, on major planning decisions?

192

(iv) Constraints
If the scope of planning is to be ambitious, the timescale long and the information available, what changes are necessary to overcome the constraints imposed by the rights of land ownership, the present tax regime, inappropriate or inadequate physical areas and the fragmentation of authority below the national level over the major public functions affecting land use?

(c) *Machinery*
In answering the following questions about the mechanics of planning it is clearly important to keep in mind both the changes in the system that have taken place since 1947, and the contrast between the large number of small developments with which it was designed to deal and the small number of large ones with which it has been obliged to cope.

(i) Have the powers and resources given to and the methods used by the various planning authorities been adequate to the range of different functions they are expected to perform?
(ii) Have these powers and resources been distributed between authorities in a coherent and effective way?
(iii) Have the boundaries of the planning authorities coincided with the relevant physical areas for planning purposes?
(iv) Have the planning authorities had access to adequate and timely information?
(v) What conflicts have arisen within planning authorities, between planning authorities, between planning authorities and other public bodies, and between planning authorities and private bodies and individuals?
(vi) What machinery exists for handling potential conflicts, including the prevention or avoidance of conflict, and how successful has it been?
(vii) How has the operation of the system been affected by the character, experience and training of those who have operated it?
(viii) What changes in powers, resources, structure, methods and means of handling conflicts would be necessary either to make good present shortcomings and/or to enable the planning system to achieve new goals and to adapt to changing circumstances in the future?

3. Method of Inquiry

The starting point of the Inquiry is doubt about what the Town and Country Planning system aims to achieve and what it can reasonably be expected to achieve. We need therefore to start with reflection and speculation rather than research.

As a first step we will *commission:*

(a) *Reflections* on the operation of the system from old planning hands with different kinds of experience, including experience abroad; and

(b) *Speculations* from iconoclasts and visionaries who can make an intelligent case for much more or much less planning, or for planning of a different kind.

Secondly we will *invite*:

(c) *Evidence* from institutions and individuals with partcular interests in and knowledge of the planning system who would like their views to be considered;

and as a third step when the main issues have been identified, we will *commission*:

(d) *Reviews* of the current state of knowledge of the planning system and related matters, about which there are no readily available authoritative accounts.

4. Reflections

A number of people with long experience of the planning system will be asked to reflect on its strengths and weaknesses, limitations and possibilities, in the light of the questions posed above. They will of course be given a free hand but it would be valuable to have their views on:

(a) *Aims*: what should the planning system be attempting to achieve;

(b) *Powers and resources*: can the deficiences of the present system be remedied for the future by changes in powers and resources, their distribution between authorities, or the creation of new planning agencies;

(c) *Techniques*: are the current techniques for planning adequate for present or future purposes and if not what other techniques are available or possible?

(d) *Forecasting*: what can be said about the likely trends in land use and in particular what are the potential land use implications and possible conflicts emerging from major national commitments, for example in the fields of energy, conservation, agriculture, forestry, housing or roads.

5. Speculations

We hope that these will be addressed to the same questions but from a more consciously radical perspective and with more emphasis on the future of the planning system.

6. Evidence

This will be solicited directly by invitation to certain bodies and persons and indirectly by a general invitation through advertisements.

7. Reviews

It is our intention to commission reviews of the current state of knowledge of various aspects of the planning system and related matters as a second stage in the Inquiry. Numerous topics immediately suggest themselves: it would be a great help if those writing reflections or speculations, or submitting evidence, could indicate the areas which they think are most important which are in most urgent need of review, or which are not adequately understood at present.

Examples of topics already suggested as suitable for review are:

(a) *Finance*: Betterment, compensation, taxation of land values etc;

(b) *Information*: the availability of adequate information on land use and land ownership;

(c) *Law and planning*: the interpretation of the law by the courts and its relation to planning practice.

(d) *Public inquiries*: their use and abuse;

(e) *The land market*: the characteristics of the market for development land and its relation to the planning system;

(f) *Iatrogenic aspects of planning*: Blight, corruption, etc;

(g) *International comparisons*: for example with US, European and Commonwealth planning;

(h) *Criticisms and alternatives*: a review of comments and proposals on the planning system since its inception;

(i) *Planning*: possible contribution of work on planning in general: what can and can't be done, including forecasting etc;

(j) *Economic theory*: contribution of economic theory on land use as such as on the general subject of governmental regulation of markets;

(k) *Impact of planning on quality of life*: an ethical overview of the stewardship and accessibility of natural resources.

Appendix II   List of Those Giving Evidence

Individuals:

J D Adshead
Elizabeth Allan
Lincoln Allison
John Anderson
Maurice Ash
R Baker
Lord Bancroft
Anthony Barker
Professor Robin Best
R Billington
J R Boddy
Walter Bor
Sir John Boynton
R G Brooke
Dr T A Broadbent
Professor M J Bruton
Sir Colin Buchanan
Sir Wilfred Burns
Professor G E Cherry
David Clark
John Collins
J B Cooper
Professor J T Coppock
Stanley Crowther
Professor J B Cullingworth
Peter Curbishley
J M Davidson
Professor D R Denman
The Rt Hon Lord Denning
Jonathan Diggines
Professor G Dix
Gari Donn
Professor David Donnison
Ernest Doubleday
Dr David Eversley
John Friend
D R Fryer
Sir Frederick Gibberd
Air Marshall Sir Michael Giddings
Malcolm Grant
Robin Grove-White

Professor Charles Haar
Nigel Haigh
David Hall
Professor Peter Hall
Michael Harloe
Dr P Healey
Sir Christopher Higgins
Dr Mayer Hillman
Geoffrey Hoard
John C Holliday
Maurice Howell
J N C James
R D Jefferies
E S Johnson
Brian Jolly
A D King
Major L C Kitching
Ian Lacey
R D Leakey
Wendy Le-Las
Professor N Lichfield
Tony Long
Philip Lowe
R M P Ludlow
Sean McConnell
Sheila McDonald
W A McKee
Richard MacRory
Professor David Mandelker
A J S Maude
J G Mejor
Lord Melchett
Nigel Moor
Sherie Naidoo
Professor Howard Newby
David Noble
Professor T O'Riordan
Professor G H Peters
Adrian Phillips
Dr Alison Ravetz
Barry Reed
W K Reilly
V Renard
J R Sandbrook
The Rev Lord Sandford
Graeme Shankland
Martin Shaw
Miss Marion Shoard
Paul Sieghart

Dr James Simmie
Professor C W Spedding
D C Stazicker
K H Storey
C V Storm
R I Stuart
Adrian Stungo
P Swann
Bernard Tennant
Harford Thomas
Andrew Thorburn
Professor Urlan Wannop
Colin Ward
J R Ware
Professor Gerald Wibberley
M V Williams
Peter Wilmott
Charles Wilson
W P Winston
Alfred Wood
I Wray
Stephen Young

Organisations:

Airfields Environment Federation (AEF)
Amey Roadstone Corporation (ARC)
Association of Consultant Planners (ACP)
Association of County Councils (ACC)
Association of District Councils (ADC)
Association of Metropolitan Authorities (AMC)
Borough of Brighton
Borough of Hove Planning Department
British Institute of Management
British Nuclear Fuels Ltd (BNFL)
Civic Trust
Confederation of British Industry (CBI)
Convention of Scottish Local Authorities (CSLA)
Council for Environmental Conservation (CoEnCo)
Council for the Protection of Rural England (CPRE)
County Planning Officers Society (CPOS)
County Planning Officers' Society of Wales (CPOSW)
Country Landowners' Association (CLA)
Devon Conservation Forum
District Planning Officers' Society (DPOS)
Greater London Council (GLC)
Hart District Council
Institute of Biology
Institute of Municipal Engineers
Institution of Environmental Health Officers (IEHO)

199

International Institute for Environment and Development
Land Decade Educational Council (LDEC)
Landscape Institute
London Boroughs Association (LBA)
London Borough of Lewisham
London Borough of Merton
London Green Belt Council
Manchester Area Council for Clean Air and Noise Control
Metropolitan Planning Officers' Society (MPOS)
National Coal Board (NCB)
National Farmers Union (NFU)
National Housing and Town Planning Council (NHTPC)
Nature Conservancy Council (NCC)
Nigel Moor & Associates
Pwllheli District Council Planning Department
Radical Institute Group (RIG)
Ramblers' Association
Royal Institute of British Architects (RIBA)
Royal Institution of Chartered Surveyors (RICS)
Royal Town Planning Institute (RTPI)
RTPI–RIBA Northern Region Joint Liaison Group
School for Advanced Urban Studies, Bristol
Society of Local Authority Chief Executives (SOLACE)
Shropshire County Council
South Yorkshire County Council
Southwark Planning Department
Town and Country-Planning Association (TCPA)
Urban Design Group (UDG)

Some organisations are referred to in the text by their initials only.

Appendix III The Objectives of Planning

The fundamental objectives of planning discussed in para 6.29 of Chapter 6 were listed in shorthand. This appendix attempts to explain and expand upon the labels there used. Each 'objective' is treated in the same sequence as it appeared in the main body of the chapter.

Environmental quality:
Refers to impacts on the quality of the physical environment or neighbourhood immediately surrounding the site upon which the land use or land fabric change is proposed—impacts on the safety, health and amenity of those using that neighbourhood.

Amenity here seems to be a function of such things as noise, pollution, smells and unsightliness or ugliness, sun and daylight quality, fresh air and privacy. Thus an activity which generates traffic or causes accidents would seem to come within the scope of town and country planning regulation. The off-site impacts are probably weighed against the on-site impacts of the land use or land fabric change—which presumably impinge on the occupier or owner.

The physical standard of living provided for the site's users:
Refers to the impact of the site-specific land use or land fabric change on the safety, health and amenity of the site's *users*, and thus on the space, circulation, construction, aesthetic and sanitary 'standards' achieved *within* the development.

The capacity of publicly supplied facilities and public expenditure:
Refers to the pressures created on the capacity of 'needed' public facilities and thus the pressure for further *public expenditure*, of the site-specific land use or land fabric change. A fairly typical question which might be asked of a development proposal, for instance, would be: will the change put increased pressure on existing schools, sewers, water supply, roads, etc and therefore produce a need to expand the capacity of public services and facilities and thus lead to further public expenditure? Developments which might lead to unusually high costs tend to receive special attention (for example, as may occur within urban sprawl).

'There is a reciprocal relationship between services and development. Development is guided to places where capacity in services exists or can most readily be provided. Conversely the planning of public services has regard to the location of existing and planned development. The basis for this approach to cost-effectiveness in service provision is provided by the system of Structure and Local planning. This framework enables the forward planning of both development and services to be coordinated.'

(Comment in submission to the inquiry by M. Shaw, Norfolk County Planning Officer)

The geographical mix of land uses and land fabrics:
Refers to the impacts on the *geographical mix* of land uses or land fabrics within the neighbourhood or region where the site-specific land use or land fabric change is located. It is often thought desirable, for example, that members of every household should have more or less equal physical access to a minimum range of certain privately and publicly supplied activities (for example, grocery shops, chemists, employment possibilities) irrespective of where they live and their access to private transport. A territorial hierarchy of different types of 'needed' activity is often discussed, with certain areas having greater needs (for example, because of lack of private transport).

The need for certain land uses and land fabrics:
Refers to the impacts on the level of provision of the particular land use being proposed or replaced, in its particular neighbourhood/region.

A frequent argument is that a neighbourhood should have a minimum level for certain land using activities or land fabrics. Usually only certain types of 'important' activity or fabric are considered essential in this respect, for example, housing, food shops, agriculture. Again, issues of *'need'* appear relevant here (especially where public sector bodies have been given the responsibility to meet the 'need' for a particular type of land fabric through public provision, for example, housing).

Conservation needs:
Refers to the impacts on *non-renewable natural and man-made resources* of the site specific land use or land fabric change. It is often thought desirable to stem the loss (including the deterioration) of land uses and land fabrics which would be difficult or at least very costly to replace or renew in the event of changes in circumstances or conditions favouring a return to the old land use or land fabric, for example, loss of high grade agricultural land to urban uses, loss of 'listed' or high grade buildings (conservation or preservation of non-renewable resources) and of sites of special 'natural' scientific interest, loss of diversity of landscapes/townscapes/habitats.

The capacity of privately supplied facilities and private expenditure:
Refers to the pressures created on the capacity of certain existing and 'needed' private facilities and thus the pressures for further off-site expenditure, of the site-specific land use or land fabric change—will the activity change put increased pressure on existing shops etc, when expansion or adaptation of such private facilities would prove extremely difficult or unusually costly (perhaps producing higher prices for consumers)?

The incidence of the 'profit' generated by the change:
Refers to the impacts of the site-specific land use or land fabric change on the *distribution* (between the developer and the 'community at large') *of the economic 'rent'* yielded by the site ('created' by the community as a whole). The local authority acting on behalf of its electorate may wish to pursue a 'community' share in the development's profitability and thus demand some form of 'planning gain'.

202

The level of competition in land use and land fabric provision:
Refers to the impacts on the level of *competition* in the provision of the land use or land fabric type being proposed or replaced in the neighbourhood as a result of the site-specific land use or land fabric change. Local authorities often wish to stem any tendency for the monopolisation of real property. Hypermarkets, for example, are often asserted to introduce an undesirable element of monopoly power in the provision of local shopping facilities—cutting prices at first to force out local traders and raising prices later on. In order to be lawful this 'objective' has generally been disguised in physical amenity terms.

Economic growth and employment:
Refers to the impacts on *economic growth* and *employment prospects* in the neighbourhood or region of the site-specific land use or land fabric change. A change of land use may, for example, reduce the level and variety of employment opportunities in the local neighbourhood. And local authorities may be more lenient on industrial 'development' proposed by small business (because of their asserted or assumed job creation potential).

Community feeling:
Refers to the impacts on *community feeling/spirit* of the site-specific land use or land fabric change. Will the change 'destroy' an established 'community' or neighbourhood?

Neighbourhood character/social balance:
Refers to the impacts on the social character or socio-economic composition and status of the site-specific land use or land fabric change. Some developments, it seems, are refused planning permission because of fears of lowering the 'social' (as well as physical) quality or tone of a neighbourhood (for example, mobile homes in established residential areas). Again such criteria are most often dressed up as physical amenity criteria to make them legal.

The provision of public infrastructure:
Refers to the *promotion of land using activities or land fabrics* which are 'needed' or demanded but *which private entrepreneurs would find extremely difficult if not impossible* to supply. Normally this refers to land uses or land fabrics which are labelled (quasi-) *'public goods'*, like parks, areas of open space and roads, where the private sector would find it very costly to exclude those people who benefited from the goods' provision and yet who decided not to pay for them. In addition there are land uses and land fabrics which are so expensive to produce and/or which become significantly cheaper to produce (in terms of per unit cost) at high production levels, that it would be unrealistic to expect any private body to produce them (especially without gaining some degree of monopoly power), for example, water supply, sewerage, and road systems.

203

Wealth redistribution:
Refers to the promotion of land use or land fabric changes which help alter the balance or relative *distribution* of the initial endowment of land and property resources, for example, grants to improve the housing stock owned by low income groups or increase the number of schools in inner city deprived areas.

Assisting property market adjustment processes:
Refers to the promotion of land use/fabric changes which would help to quicken up *market adjustment* processes in order to overcome, say, problems of excess demand for land uses or land fabrics. The Community Land Act, for instance, was often used by local authorities (in giving them wider powers of land purchase) to encourage the release of land held by recalcitrant land owners who appeared to be holding up the development process unnecessarily.

Urban renewal:
Refers to the promotion of land fabric renewal where only the financial costs associated with demolition and land assembly act as an obstacle to redevelopment and where the existing land fabric and land ownership pattern is having a deleterious impact on the safety, health or amenity of these using the site and its neighbourhood.

5.12/13

8.4

9.40

Social costs   9.18